Damn Son Where Did You Find This?*

*A signature sample used by mixtape artist Trap-A-Holics.

Author's Note

Having always operated in a legal grey zone, where mixtapes were hustled on the streets to build temporary hype, the hiphop mixtape scene went digital over the past decade. But its underground nature has remained even as mixtapes became an exclusively online phenomenon. As web servers expire or get shut down by the authorities, mixtapes have stayed just as temporal on the internet as they were when they were being sold on street corners.

With very few people putting value into the preservation of the chaotic and fast-moving world of hiphop mixtapes, a vast majority of releases are doomed to be forgotten as soon as hard drives get cleaned or crash. Along with all of the music, the incredible treasures of mixtape cover artwork, which are often more memorable than the music that they represent, disappear. Mixtape cover art is one of the, if not the most, unique visual worlds to develop since the computer began dominating graphic design 30 years ago. Thanks to the vacuum of regulation that the mixtape market operates in, the artwork of mixtape covers has evolved into what you will see in the coming pages; an extreme form of visual communication, unapologetic in its nature, where the name of the game is to turn heads and grab attention. Absent are the *Parental Advisory* stickers or strict criteria that must be met to get an album on Walmart's shelves, creating an aesthetic with zero restrictions on explicit content, sexuality, drug references or graphic violence. But mixtape artwork is so much more than that.

This book was inspired by our love and appreciation for the extensive environments that live in the square canvases of mixtape covers. Its intent is to capture and preserve a surrealistic and grand era, starting in the early 00s, when mixtape covers' reflection of contemporary pop culture, politics, and internal affairs reached new heights.

The dreams of luxurious lifestyles, altered film posters where *Toy Story* transforms into *Trap Story,* lyrical altercations between rappers imagined through the brutal world of the *Street Fighter* video games. The mixtape designers which we have chosen to profile are wizards of Adobe Photoshop who can transform fragments of stock imagery into a coherently colored scene of a car chase with bullets flying through the air, all done within the timeframe of a few hours and for as little as a couple hundred dollars. With hundreds, or even thousands, of unique covers to their names, the designers which we have selected have made an exception to the rule that quantity comprises quality. They serve as the perfect example of the heroes that built their underground culture into their own art world.

It's a boys' world, with men being the majority involved in this niche of the graphic design industry. But just as the world of hiphop is finally beginning to open itself up in terms of wider social acceptance, we can't wait to see what future female mixtape designers will do for a new era of gay rappers and other norm-breaking hiphop artists.

Our book stands as a documentation of this recent phenomenon in hiphop culture, covering an epic era in mixtape history. But foremost, it is a tribute to all of the designers that spent countless hours behind their computers crafting an artform as far away from the traditional art world as you can get. We are confident that this unique form and style will inspire designers, artists, and art directors in the future.

Tobias Hansson
Stockholm, December 2014.

Michael Thorsby
Paris, December 2014.

Introduction

Mixtapes have always been an important part of the hiphop industry, for artists, labels, and fans alike. Since the birth of the genre in the late 80s and early 90s, the independent and underground culture of mixtapes has been just as instrumental to the evolution of hiphop as the major label efforts that brought the music into the mainstream. Over the years, mixtapes have taken many different forms to serve various purposes. At first, there were the homemade mixtapes on cassettes (which gave them a name that stuck even as CDs and digital versions took over) for personal consumption and sharing with friends, which DJ and mixtape entrepreneur Trap-A-Holics remembers from his youth. *I used to record DJ Clue's radio show 'Mixtape Mondays' faithfully. Every Monday night, I knew he was going to play exclusive music that I've never heard before.* Rob Markman, a hiphop writer and critic who has worked for MTV News, XXL, The Source and Complex, shares similar memories of his first encounters with mixtapes. *When we were kids, me and my friends used to write a list of songs that we wanted to get on the tape and just wait by the radio all day and make our own mixtapes. A lot of kids did that.*

But not every fan had the time to wait at the radio all day to create their perfect tape, so there came professional distributors of mixtapes to meet the demand in the streets for the latest and greatest tracks. *We would go to the Fulton Mall in Brooklyn where there were little stands that sold sneakers and hats and tapes,* Rob Markman recalls. *There was also the bootleggers who just put a blanket on the street corner. Sometimes the stores couldn't get the real mixtapes, so we'd buy the bootleg ones. Whenever I wanted a tape, I never had a problem. I'd just go to the guy on the corner, pick a tape, and keep moving. It wasn't just mixtapes though, they'd sell you a bootleg copy of Nas's 'Illmatic', too.*

Mixtapes didn't only work as a form of playlist-making and pre-internet music piracy, but also as an avenue for up-and-coming rappers to gain exposure, which they're still used for today. *Rappers used to make demo tapes and send it to the label, but you usually just ended up in a box, nobody would ever listen to you* Markman explains. *But with mixtapes, you put it out and marketed it yourself and then the labels came to you. I can't think of an artist who got signed recently that hasn't put out a mixtape. The mixtape is the new demo.*

While the mixtape culture was lively in New York, it was the South that played the most important role in the evolution of the format. As hiphop came to the mainstream in the 90s, major labels only seemed to be signing artists from New York and Los Angeles, leaving countless MCs and DJs from the rest of America struggling to be heard. Having accepted that A&Rs weren't interested in any non-East/West Coast rappers, Southern artists turned to mixtapes to create their own industry and launched themselves into stardom without any assistance from the music industry. When the record labels finally took notice of the vibrant Southern mixtape culture, many rappers weren't even interested in signing recording deals, such as Slim Thug, who turned down his first major label offer because of the satisfaction that his mixtape career had brought him. It was mixtape distributors such as Evil Empire and Trap-A-Holics, not major labels, that brought the Southern mixtape stars to a national audience. *At the time, the South was really emerging as the 'it' region of hiphop. Young Jeezy, Rick Ross, Lil Wayne. We just decided we need to capitalize on that first.*

Trap-A-Holics also found success through the Southern culture of mixtapes, producing mixtapes for such artists as Gucci Mane, Lil Boosie, Waka Flocka Flame and Juicy J. *I saw how the south started bubbling up. I just felt a void that was missing from the game, which was that trap element that I grew up with. I just wanted to create a little name, so I started doing mixtapes on my own to try to put music out for the people to hear. We came up from nothing, just a bunch of kids from Connecticut and Atlanta, grinding and hustling and putting it all together.*

Though releasing mixtapes may have begun as a way to get a major label record deal, the careers of Southern mixtape MCs has helped the format take on a life of its own over the years, becoming arguably as important to the genre as retail albums. Unsatisfied with the waiting time between major releases, even the most successful rappers continued putting out mixtapes to remain relevant and comment on the happenings of the culture. *They were creating these mixtapes that were kind of like albums because we consumed them like albums, but they weren't quite albums,* Markman says. *The magazines and the media had to catch up, you couldn't ignore it because everybody in the streets was talking about it.*

The mixtape format also allowed artists to take risks that they weren't able to with their commercial releases. *Mixtapes definitely became over-the-top and super creative. Rappers could put out things that they couldn't do on an album, things that labels wouldn't let them do. Nas is a perfect example, he wanted to put out an album called 'Nigger' but Def Jam said no. So he put out a mixtape with that name. What he wasn't allowed to do on an album, he could do on a mixtape.* The mixtape represented freedom for both rappers and fans. Established rappers had a platform to put out music without interference from their label, undiscovered rappers had the freedom to be heard without going through the traditional channels of the industry, and fans had the freedom to hear the hottest new music.

Soon enough, an entire industry arose, with countless sources producing and distributing mixtapes on the streets, both legally and illegally. Trap-A-Holics, who became one of the most successful DJs and distributors in the mixtape industry, remembers the early days of his career, *I used to wake up, do my little mixtape, and run around Connecticut and New York in a car with thousands of CDs in the trunk, just selling them from store to store. I would get 5 dollars per mixtape, so if I sold you five hundred, I would have been able to go home and call it a day. Nowadays, I would be lucky if I get to a quarter of that. The internet killed the gas station mixtape. You can download them anywhere at any given moment and you don't have to pay one red penny.*

New technologies have been shaping the mixtape world since its birth, whether it be more rappers being able to self-produce their music, more distributors being able to mass-produce physical copies, or the internet allowing widespread digital distribution of a growing number of mixtapes. But the most noticeable innovation might have nothing to do with the music being packaged into the mixtapes, but rather the packaging itself. Mixtape cover art has gone through a drastic evolution over the past two decades, generating a unique aesthetic unlike anything else in music and generating countless pieces of art within it.

I was always fascinated by mixtape art, prolific mixtape producer Evil Empire says. *It's all about the artwork, because that's what the consumer sees first. They are looking at a hundred other mixtapes, everybody's putting out mixtapes, so it comes down to the artwork and who has the best. Nine times out of ten, the consumer is going to pick up something with a cover that looks more appealing to them. That's why the cover is one of the most important things when putting out a project. Having your artwork stick out better than any other mixtape.*

In the heavily saturated and competitive mixtape industry, cover art has become almost as important as the music itself, with rappers and DJs fighting to get the best designs that can catch people's attention enough to get their music heard. This constant search for the best cover art has contributed to the development of the mixtape design aesthetic, flashy, chaotic, and maximalistic fantasy worlds, all trying to one-up each other to be the most compelling cover on the shelf (or the site). But mixtapes didn't always have this signature style of larger-than-life Photoshop collages that reflected the fairytale street worlds described in rappers' lyrics. Rob Markman reflects the early days, before distributors started to prioritize the cover art of the their product and their unique aesthetic came to form in the 00s.
There wasn't much of a style back when you bought the bootlegs. Sometimes it was just a neon orange cover and it just said 'DJ Clue'. The early mixtape covers looked disgusting, but

for better or worse, that's kind of what attracted me to them, when they'd just put the track listing on the front. The covers looked like shit, but if I could count to five songs that I want off of it, it was worth my five dollars. They were the shittiest mixtapes covers, but a lot of my favorite mixtapes had these covers.

As the market became more competitive and new technologies allowed mixtape producers to acquire cheap graphic design, distributors increasingly focused on the visuals of their mixtapes, unable to rely on simply having the hottest tracks. *Initially, mixtape cover artwork was pretty laughable,* cover art collector Mixtape Wall says. *It was far-fetched. It was weird to me. But at the same time, there was an aesthetic to it that I really liked.*

When graphic design tools like Photoshop became easier to access, rappers and DJs were given unprecedented opportunities to obtain professional looking cover art for their mixtapes, which they quickly exploited to the fullest. And given that everything in the mixtape world is, as Evil Empire admits, *technically not legal,* the boundaries of the mixtape cover medium were pushed as far as possible until the design side of a mixtape's development became almost as exciting as the music.

The thing I love is when I ask a graphic designer to do, say, ten covers for me. I just can't wait to get those covers back to see what they look like, Evil Empire explains. *When the covers come back and they're exactly what I wanted, I'm just like 'yes, cool, these tapes are going to move. These tapes are going to do what they're supposed to do'.*

With mixtapes design, the sky's the limit, Mixtape Wall says. *You can get any visual you want if you'll pay a designer for it. Since the mixtapes are not technically being sold, you're not violating any laws. Or maybe you are, but nobody cares about it. You can just download any visuals and design, whatever you want.*

The freedom that rappers and DJs were granted in their designs turned mixtape covers into an expressive medium as effective as the rhymes themselves. *What makes a good mixtape cover is your initial reaction. You look at it and it makes you look even closer. There's storytelling in the cover,* Mixtape Wall explains. *From what I've seen, and this is what I like about mixtape covers, mixtape covers can be like rappers. They're really sensitive. If you comment on their shoes, they'll get furious and write a song about you. So a lot of people will use their covers to take on current events in the same way.*

I've done movie based covers, where we take a movie poster and turn it into a mixtape cover, Evil Empire recalls. *Maybe take an old album cover and turn it into a mixtape cover. Like for 'Coke Boyz 3', we took the whole N.W.A. theme from their 'Greatest Hits' cover and re-did it. With current events, we did a Young Jeezy cover called 'American Dream' which had the whole presidency theme to it. That was around the time he came out with 'My President is Black'.*

The unbounded nature of mixtape cover design has caused problems for rappers and distributors, as their covers began to upset people in the mainstream who saw their images being re-purposed into the outrageous and often controversial aesthetic of mixtape art. *I did a 'Tennessee Titans' tape and I used the Titans' official NFL logo,* Trap-A-Holics admits. *Two days later, I received an official letter from Roger Goodell of the National Football League saying, 'Listen, take this off or we are going to sue your ass'. I was scared. I told my boy 'take this off'. So when I started seeing that, I knew that we were making noise and that we had touched a nerve. We were on to something. And this was 2008. To this day, the NFL still sends me letters.*

As mixtape covers began taking on current events, they increasingly became a form of communication on their own, as artists became well aware that their cover art could be a more effective medium to send a message than the lyrics in their music. Rappers and DJs releasing several mixtapes per year started using their covers to comment on what was happening in hiphop culture, often dissing each other back and forth with each new mixtape. *Mixtape covers now don't last long. They have a really short life span,* says Mixtape Wall. *It's maybe a month before they're out of style. But some covers, you just remember. I don't remember the music but I remember seeing it online or in a magazine or in an actual store years ago. That's the purpose, to draw peoples attention to notice and download it.*

In the sea of mixtapes fighting to gain attention, some covers have become timeless for their impact on the greater hiphop culture. Both Mixtape Wall and Evil Empire bring up the particularly memorable cover for a Rick Ross and 50 Cent mixtape called *Kiss My Pinky Ring,* which Evil Empire distributed himself. *One of my favorite covers was that design by KidEight,* Mixtape Wall says. *He had Rick Ross as a police officer and 50 Cent as a clown wearing that curly wig. Stuff like that I find hilarious.*

This was when 50 Cent and Rick Ross were going through their beef, Evil Empire explains. *So on the cover, we called them 'Pimpin' Curly' and 'Officer Ricky.' We had Rick Ross done like a cop eating donuts. That wasn't my idea, that was KidEight's idea. 50 Cent started going in on Rick Ross and putting that cover in the end of all his videos when he was doing his 'This Is 50' web series. I didn't put my name on the cover because it was too controversial and it wasn't an official mixtape. But that one definitely put KidEight on the map and got a lot of people reaching out to him.*

Despite the impact that mixtape covers have had on the entire hiphop industry and its evolution, the graphic designers behind them rarely get the attention or credit that they deserve for their work. Though their designs play a key role in getting a mixtape to the ears of hundreds of thousands of listeners, their financial compensation is surprisingly low, forcing the designers to complete dozens of projects per month to make a living.

While many mixtape designers are genuine hiphop fans using their Photoshop skills to participate in the culture, the industry is also full of skilled graphic designers who aspire to work with more lucrative commercial work. *If you ask any designer about their dream project, they'll say one of two things, either to design a movie poster or to design an album cover,* Mixtape Wall explains. *And honestly, the odds are that you won't do either. Therefore, the mixtape cover is the closest thing. They get to design a cover. It may not be a retail album but it's the second best thing.*

For those designers still generating endless amounts of covers, it's important that they receive the attention that they deserve for the work that's been so important to hiphop as a whole. While many might see mixtape art as a formulaic medium with seemingly cookie-cutter designs, there are a handful of designers who have developed a signature style that might go unnoticed in the overwhelming flow of new mixtapes. *To the normal eye, all of these designs might seem the same. But to me, they're not similar at all,* Evil Empire says. *As far as the images, the style and the way the text is placed, these designers are totally different.*

To gain a new perspective on the incomparable art of mixtape covers and the unique world behind it, we've spoken with five of the industry's top graphic designers, KidEight, Miami Kaos, Mike Rev, Tansta and Skrilla and we've asked them how they see their craft and this culture from their diverse perspectives.

KidEight

Gucci Mane
Ice Cream Man

While technology's effect on the mixtape world is impossible to ignore, KidEight serves as a perfect example of just how much the culture has evolved through the age of the internet. Not only did KidEight become one of the most sought-out graphic designers in hiphop while he was still a teenager, but he did so without ever setting foot in the United States. Nearly a decade since he began doing graphic design, UK native KidEight still haven't ever been across the Atlantic, despite having become such an important figure in the visual world of US hiphop. *I plan to go every year but time just roll by. I'm always too busy. I find it funny really. The thought that some white kid from England can be the go-to guy for a lot of US trap rappers sounds hilarious to me.*

At a young age, KidEight had already immersed himself in art at the encouragement of his parents. *I started doing art even before I could read. The house that I was raised in had a cellar. It was dark and damp and no one really went there, but my mum gave me some paint and let me do what I wanted down there. The cellar had two rooms, one my mum used as a dark room to develop photos, the other was where I was allowed to paint.* KidEight spent hours in his family's cellar, covering the walls with his artistic explorations, a hobby that would later lead him to start writing graffiti at the age of 13.

Around the same time as he brought his artistic ambitions out of the cellar and into the streets, his uncle gave him cracked copies of Adobe Photoshop 5.5, Flash and Dreamweaver. It lead him to begin experimenting with graphic design. *I started doing web design at around the age of 14 and got my first paid website job when I was 15. I left home the year after to go to school and studied fine art and graphic design for a year and half. But soon I really started hating it. I felt I wasn't learning anything and it was a waste of time. This was around the same time that MySpace was taking off. I set up a page offering web and graphic design and got a few clients that way.*

KidEight's big break came when PDA, an established mixtape cover designer, took notice of the young artist's skills in the mid 00s. *PDA was in the process of getting out of the graphic game to move into photography. I guess he liked my work and referred me to two or three of his steady clients.* KidEight doesn't view this event as PDA simply passing him the torch, though. *I had to prove my work was up to par.* KidEight quickly gained notoriety amongst rappers and other graphic designers and before long he was designing mixtape covers full time. *When I started, internet forums were a lot more active. I got in contact with a lot of designers that way. The way I see it, what we're doing is kind of nerdy. We all spend many hours of our lives in front of computers, cutting and pasting photos of rappers for money. It's isolating, doing work by myself at home. So I like to talk to like-minded people whenever possible.* Even though his work is done mostly in solitude, KidEight has managed to integrate himself into the US industry as much as he can from his UK home. For a period, he even set up a forum called PSTrappin.com solely dedicated to mixtape design and designers. Henceforth, the name included the PS abbreviation of Photoshop, rarely used by other than graphic design professionals. *I haven't had time to maintain the forum, but through it, I've connected with many talented artists such as Proph Bundy, Jay Goldz, Mr. Soul from ATL. Before that, I chatted online with Tansta a couple of times. I speak to Miami Kaos whenever we catch each other on Twitter. Deftone and I used to email weekly and I've stayed in contact with MeF Designs from Australia on a weekly basis for the last five years. I think without him, I'd probably have quit.*

Within the mixtape design community, KidEight has grown into a respected and highly influential figure. When asked if he sees himself as a trendsetter in the industry, he remains humble. *I think I've created a few trends unintentionally. But it's impossible to decide, 'Okay, I'm going to create a trend.' You just try something until it works. If enough people see it working, they will follow.* On the subject of his followers and competition, KidEight remains sensible and seems to not have an ego. *I think all mixtape designers borrow from each other. When I started, it was a small community. We all knew of each other and, in some cases, spoke on social media or through chat clients. I was always of the belief that if you pull together, you can share the wealth. If I had a certain resource someone wanted, I'd have no issues in sharing and in return I'd like to think that others were the same.*

With his strong work ethic, KidEight has become one of the most prolific designers in hiphop, creating more covers than he can even keep track of. *It has to be near 3000 now, since 2007,* he guesses. Despite his success, KidEight remains realistic about his career. *Sometimes when I do sit down and think about it, I get anxious that the bubble might burst. But I'm seven years strong now with no signs of work slowing down.* When reflecting on his career and where it will go next, he remains pragmatic in his perspective. *Mixtapes have been good to me but I've always had my fingers in other pies. I think a lot of people see mixtape design as a lesser form of design but I love it with all my heart. Mixtapes have allowed me to build a client base of people from around the world, a lot of which I would call friends. Also, not to sound big-headed because I hate all that, but it has paid me extremely well. At the age of 24, I've been able to buy two houses and live a lifestyle that I could only have dreamed of when I started seven years ago.*

Besides his professional success, what's most striking about KidEight is the genuine love that he has for his work. When discussing a popular cover that he created for a Ransom & DJ Drama mixtape, KidEight proudly lists the high number of views, downloads and streams that the tape received and acknowledges how it became DatPiff.com's most downloaded mixtape by an independent artist. But what pleases him the most is how his cover was received by his clients. *They loved my design, which for me is the most important part.*

KidEight now balances his mixtape cover designing with other projects including web design and working as an in-house designer for VladTV.com and SneakWatch.com. He's also designed online media campaigns for LiveMixtapes.com and WorldStarHipHop.com, as well as his first DVD cover for the film *Birds of a Feather*, starring Zaytoven, Al Nuke, Gucci Mane and Big Bank Black. *I think if you make too many plans, you set yourself up for a fall. I've seen a lot of mixtape designers make a big deal of leaving the game and not doing mixtapes anymore. But they always end up coming back. All I want to be is a designer, whether it be mixtapes, corporate shop fronts, or whatever. As long as I have the freedom to be my own boss and do what I love, I'm happy.*

Please describe your creative process. How do you come up with your concepts?

Well, concepts are something that I like to discuss with clients. These days, so many titles are things like *The Turn Up* and *Swag This, Swag That*. Basically slang terms. Slang is subjective to what area of the world or the USA that you're in, so getting ideas from something that is different to everyone is near impossible. Concepts can be the biggest headache. Often you'll ask a client and their reply will be very little help. A running joke amongst designers is *make it hood*, which really offers no help but seems to be a reply we all get. The worst is when you go ahead and do what you feel, and then the client will describe to you exactly what they want when they reject your draft.

DJ Fletch & Young Jeezy
Medellin Music

Project Pat & DJ Scream
Cheez 'N Dope

Juvenile
Deliquency

DJ Fletch & OJ Da Juiceman
Juice On The Loose 3

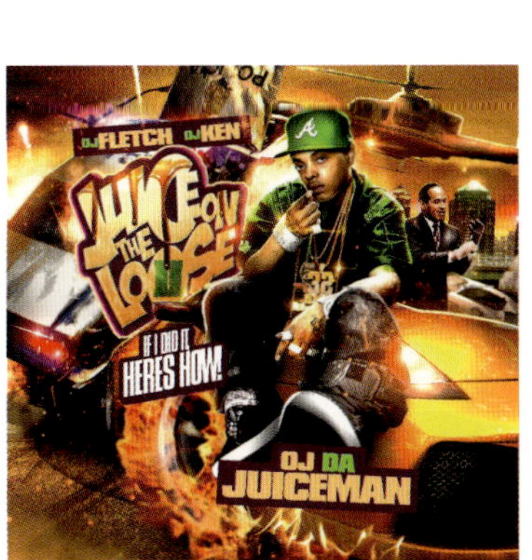

DJ Fletch, DJ Ken & OJ Da Juiceman
Juice On The Loose 2

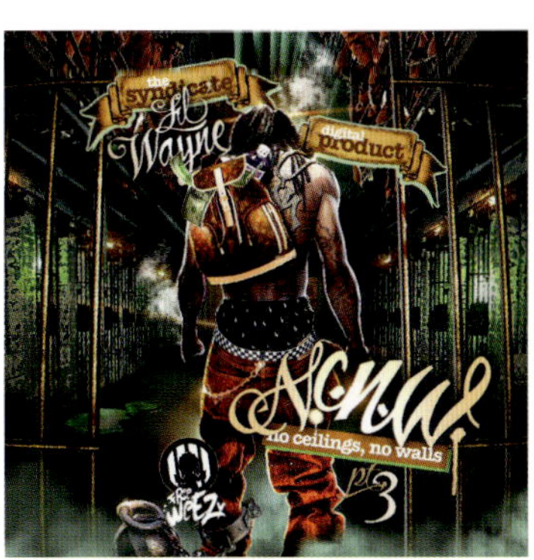

Lil Wayne
N.C.N.W. – No Ceilings, No Walls Pt.3

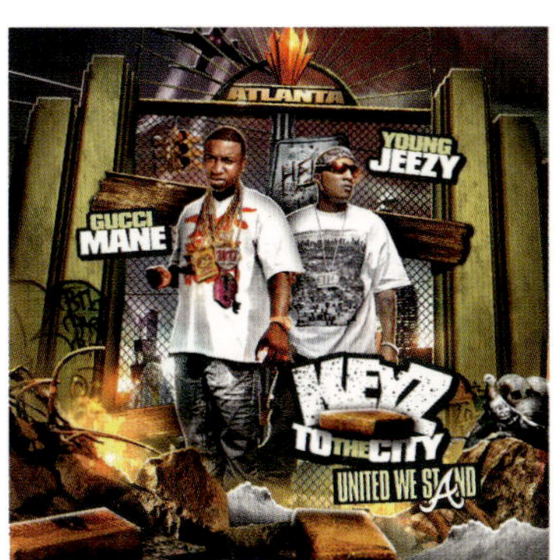

Gucci Mane & Young Jeezy
Keyz To The City – United We Stand

The Syndicate & Lil Wayne
No Ceilings No Walls

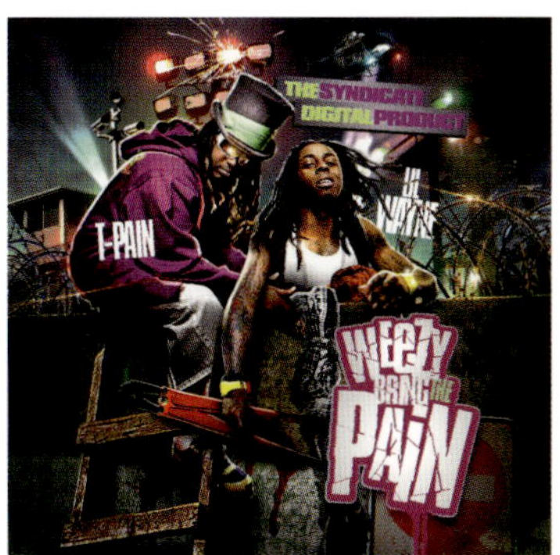

The Syndicate, T-Pain & Lil Wayne
Weezy Bring The Pain

DJ Haze & DJ Hood
Blood Is Thicker Than Water XVI

The Syndicate & Lil Wayne
Hell's Kitchen

DJ Drama, DJ Scream, DJ Whoo Kid & Shawty Lo
Fright Night

DJ Woogie & Mr Peter Parker
3 Headed Monster

DJ Drama & Fabolous
There Is No Competition 2 – The Funeral Service

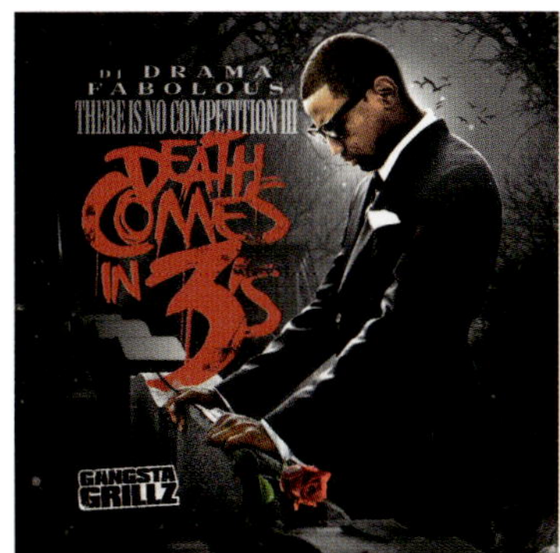

DJ Drama & Fabolous
There Is No Competition 3 – Death Comes In 3's

DJ Fletch & Tupac Shakur
Life After Death

Trap Squad
Trappin Aint Dead

DJ Scream, DJ Smallz & Young Buck
*Back On My Buck Sh*t 2*

Riot Squad present Chinx Drugz
Hurry Up And Die

Rick Ross & Tapemasters Inc.
Illustrious Pt.2

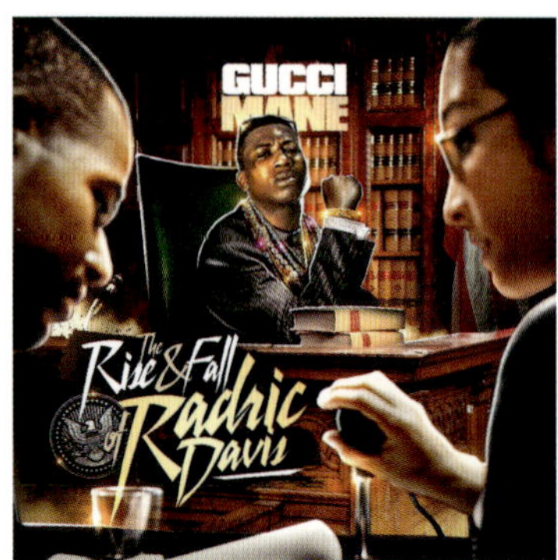

Gucci Mane
The Rise & Fall Of Radric Davis

DJ Prophecy
DFB – Deep Fried Blends 4

Ihatemixtapes presents
Dope Boy Swag 2

Trina
*5 Star B*tch*

Gucci Mane & Waka Flocka Flame
Ferrari Boyz

Plies & Rick Ross
Goons Wit Attitudes

Tapemasters Inc. & Lloyd Banks
City Of Dreams

Hustle University presents Young R
Billion Dollar Dreams

Tapemasters Inc. & 2 Chainz
24 Karats

Meek Mill
Motivation

DJ Smallz & DJ Shure Fire
#First Class – It's Not a Section, It's a Lifestyle

Cam'ron, DJ Drama & Vado
Boss of All Bosses 2

Tapemasters Inc. & DJ Envy
Purple Codeine 32

Tapemasters Inc. & DJ Envy
Purple Codeine 27

Tapemasters Inc.
Purple Codeine 38

Do DJs ever ask you to come up with the concept or the title of the tape?

The DJ and compilation tapes are usually a home run. I get a lot more creative freedom on series like *Street Runnaz* by DJ Spinatik, or like the old *Modern Day Marvel* series from 2008. I usually get told to do my thing on those and there's usually never any issues.

Do you prefer creative freedom or limitations?

It depends on the project. Freedom is good, but only if the client means it. I have a client that tells me to be different on nearly everything we do, but he always hates what I do and wants to go back to generic, regurgitated ideas. I think what's more important for me is that the client is happy at the end of the project. I've fallen out with a few people in the past because I've tried to guide them towards the direction I see fitting the project.

That's interesting because your look is very personal. It's not noticeable that there are many compromises.

I like to put my stamp on my work, without a doubt, but there are always compromises.

Do you keep versions of what you prefer the cover to be?

Yeah, a lot of times if it's something I liked more than the final, I'll put that on my portfolio.

Can you describe the feeling when you designed your first mixtape and saw it out on the market?

Well, I rarely get a chance to physically see my work with me being in England. But I guess my first proper mixtape job was for a local artist. It was a full retail release so it was my first time having to work with print guidelines, et cetera. It was good to hold something like that in my hands but I never got paid so... mixed emotions.

What tools do you use? Is your process fully digital or do you also sketch by hand?

I'm basically fully digital. My current set up is new generation Macbook plugged into a iMac with a 27 inch screen, used as secondary screen. Along with that I have a couple of external hard drives and an Apple Mighty Mouse. That's what I use on a daily basis. Sometimes, for logos, I sketch by hand before I get into the computer but mostly I start with Adobe Illustrator straight away.

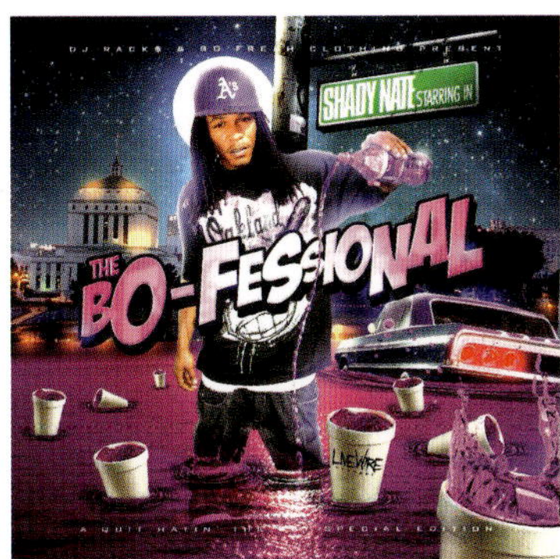

DJ Rack$ & So Fresh Clothing present Shady Nate
The Bo-Fessional

J-Money, Dr Scream & Dr Holiday
The Medication

Young Dro & Yung LA
LA Dro

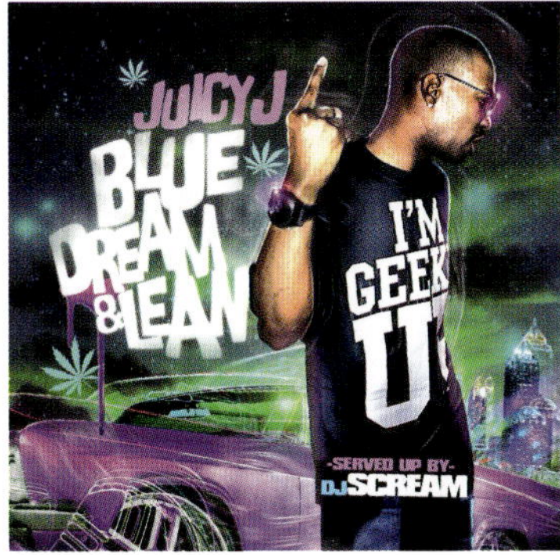

Juicy J & DJ Scream
Blue Dream & Lean

Tapemasters Inc. & Wiz Khalifa
House Party

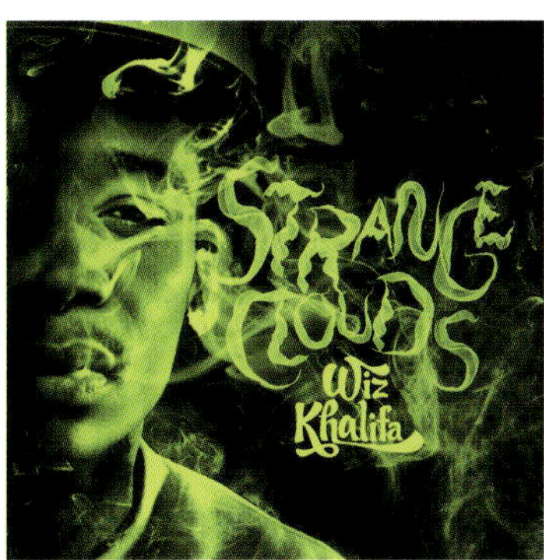

Wiz Khalifa
Strange Clouds

In general, how much time do you allow yourself to spend on a cover?

Some covers are an hour. Others can be three to four. When I started, every cover was four to five hours.

During your most creative periods, how many mixtape covers have you been producing per month?

I would say in the last 30 days, I have probably done 70. But I have done 18 in two days a couple of times. It really depends on circumstances.

How important is it that the music and artwork correlate?

I personally feel that the music and art should always fit together. That's one of my biggest problems when trying to talk to certain clients. I hate to say it but a lot of rappers aren't original and will probably never make it. Too many people want to ride other people's wave. For example, whenever Kanye drops a project, people flood to you asking you to *make it like Kanye*. When I did Juicy J's *Blue Dreams & Lean*, I had people coming to me daily saying, *make it like Juicy J's*. When Mike Rev did Meek Mill's *Dreamchasers 2*, all any designer heard for months was *make it like Meek Mill's cover*. Just because another rapper has a buzz or a style doesn't mean you have to try to replicate it. Originality stands alone.

And how do you create a clear connection between the music and the cover? Do you try to capture an energy? Expand on subjects from the lyrics? Or anything else?

It's easier when it's an artist whose music you've heard before. Recently, the rapper Ransom has been putting out a lot more projects. I've been a fan of his music for years so I know the best look for him. When I did *Astronaut Status* for Future, I'd already done a couple more covers for him so I was starting to work out what kind of style worked for him. I find it hard when I've never heard an artist's music. When it's someone I'm unfamiliar with, I will always try to ask them what they're about, what they talk about. A lot of times, the passion in their response can guide me in the right direction.

There's a lot more simple covers around now. Do you think it's a change of direction because clients want to pay less?

Simple isn't necessarily bad. I like simple covers. I just don't like graphically bad covers. Now anyone can download Photoshop and become a *designer*. All you have to do is to

DJ Fletch & Plies
Top Goon

Nicki Minaj, DJ Gutta & Haris Amilli
The Exorcism Of Roman Zolanski

MARVEL
DJ DECKO
DJ LAZY K
PRESENTS
#8
CTE
CORPORATE THUGZ ENTERTAINMENT
MIXRUS.COM
YOUNG
JEEZY
STARRING AS
HULK
modern day
marvels
LAZY K PRODUCTIONS

DJ Decko, DJ Lazy K present Jay-Z
Modern Day Marvels – Batman

DJ Decko, DJ Lazy K present Raekwon
Modern Day Marvels – Dr. Doom

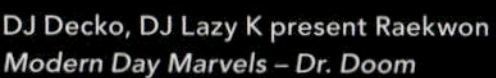

DJ Fletch presents Gorilla Zoe
G.I. Zoe – A True American Hero

Nicki Minaj
Barbie World

DJ Fletch & Gunplay
Megatron

Gucci Mane & DJ Drama
The Burrprint – The Movie 3-D

DJ Gutta, DJ Diggz, DJ Lust & DJ Bchenk
King Kong Returns

32 Ent & Cannonmusic, OJ Da Juiceman & Don Cannon
The Lord Of The Rings

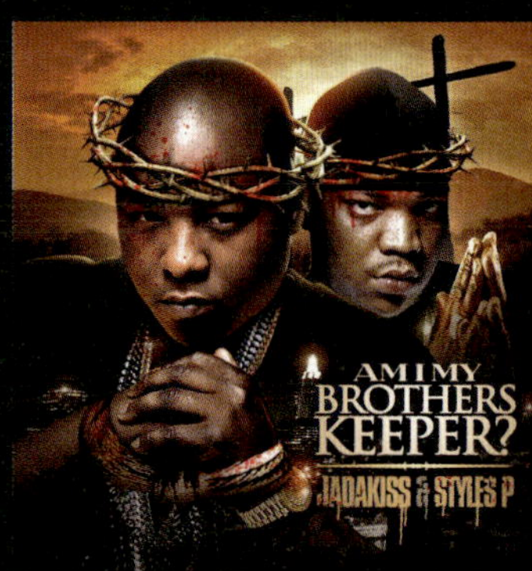

Jadakiss & Styles P
Am I My Brother's Keeper?

DJ Fletch & Gorilla Zoe
Planet Of The Apes

Lil Scrappy & DJ Scream
Suicide

Maybach Music, Bilderburg Group & Commission
presents Gunplay & DJ Holiday – *Caligula*

Lil Wayne
The Blue Martian

Darkage Ent & Mel Funk
Funk All Ya'll

get on Instagram or Twitter. A rapper ask *who does graphic design?* through social media and hundreds of people will reply who have no portfolio, credentials, or experience. I'm happy that I came up when I did and not now.

How do you feel about the competition between graphic designers in the mixtape industry? It seems like there's some pretty ruthless competition.

Well, it seems that way. It's not how I like it. Mixtape design is so isolated from other design and it's a grey area in many senses. In other industries, if someone outright bites your work, you could sue them. With mixtapes, you have to charge it to the game and do your best to make your work even better than before. Use it as inspiration and try to move further past the competition. I couldn't tell you who was the first to use lens flares in covers but we all do now. I have folders of covers that I've done which have been completely bitten and ripped off by other designs, but what can I do? Getting pissed off and calling out the designer doesn't do a thing. With graffiti, if you copy or bite when you make a piece, you'll get your work lined out and probably get beaten if you ever get caught. Try doing that on the internet!

DJ Fletch & Gucci Mane
Gucci Gone Bonkers

How would you say your past in graffiti has influenced you as a graphic designer in general and your mixtape covers in particular?

I definitely think there is a link. Graffiti is a form of typography. Type is as important in mixtape covers as any other photographic or illustrated element. I also think that my use of colours and understanding of swatches helped. When you do a graffiti piece, you want it to be noticed. Knowing what colours work well together and stand out helps your work get noticed and that applies to both graffiti and when you design mixtape covers.

Your way of working with colours is very striking. Is it a deliberate process or based on intuition?

I'm not even sure. My earlier mixtape covers were especially striking. I used to work hours on getting the colours to pop in a way that I didn't think anyone else was at the time. To be honest, I didn't know Photoshop to the level that I do now, so it was a lot of trial and error. In recent years, I've learned to make adjustment layers. But ultimately, I believe you really need to have an eye for colours. For example, I know exactly what shade of purple I want to use in a skyline and I know the exact color code of orange that will work perfectly with it.

EVIL EMPIRE & DJ FLETCH PRESENT
WELCOME
TO Fabulous
LAS VEGA
NEVADA
THE HANGOVER
STARRING GUCCI MANE & OJ DA JUICEMAN
2 CD & DVD SPECIAL EDITION

Trap-A-Holics
T.W.O. – Trap World Order

DJ Jmas
Area 51 4

Rick Ross
*F*ck The Rap Game*

Drake
Heartbreak Drake – The Graduation

Drake
Heartbrake Drake – The High Honors 4.0

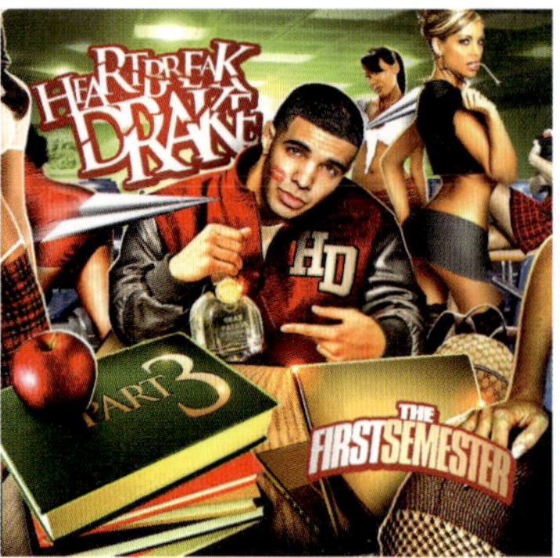

Drake
Heartbrake Drake – The First Semester Part 3

Do you sometimes draw inspiration from real life, while being out in the city or nature? Or do you draw up these palettes from sheer imagination?

There has been times when I'll be away from the computer and I'll notice a certain way that light may shine on a person and how it behaves on different surfaces. How skin may absorb light a certain way. I used to pick perhaps five colours that I knew I wanted to work into a design before I started. Now I try not to constrain myself so much.

You mention how the colours pop. Another thing that make your covers pop are your work with highlights. How would you describe your usage of highlights?

I can't fully take credit for the highlights. I remember that a couple of designers started using it before me. Deftone and Tansta. But I think we all used it in different ways. It got to the point a few years ago where everyone started using it without really understanding what we were trying to achieve. A rim light is a light that is placed directly behind a figure. It will almost outline the person depending on their clothing, accessories, et cetera. It's supposed to give the piece depth but a lot of times it can just make the person look like a cardboard cut out.

You show a lot of imagination in the concepts you create and you're very good at drawing up cinematic scenes. Where does this come from?

I watch a lot of movies. I actually watch more movies than I listen to music. I guess movie posters are my biggest inspiration. Every part of them appeals to me. I suppose I'm trying to bring to mixtapes what movie posters are to the actual movie.

Tansta said that he no longer put stacks of cash on the ground in the street because it's *unrealistic*. Are there any similar things you wouldn't do?

I've never thought any of that was realistic. I think it's all about balance. More than often, the client will request stuff like that. My old style was kind of known for being cartoony. I've done all kinds of crazy things on covers that aren't realistic. Sometimes covers are like panels in a comic book, they don't have to always be realistic.

There was a time when all mixtape covers seemed to be influenced by current events, like the 2008 presidential election, Hurricane Katrina, et cetera. This is one of the more interesting sides of mixtape culture but it seems like it is fading away. Why do you think that is?

Plies & DJ Scream
You Need People Like Me Pt.2

Plies & DJ Scream
You Need People Like Me

Yes, I see that too and it's something I miss a lot. I really think it stems from mixtapes changing as a whole. The way I understand it, DJs no longer sell units like they used to. Compilation tapes are now a vehicle for a DJ to push himself as a host for parties or an independent artist host. Gone are the days of standing out on a rack by having the best artwork. Now it's all about the price. The bigger DJs will get free work or covers for very cheap. This means that younger designs are basically whoring themselves out for 30 dollars. People used to take pride in their craft. Now, not so much. I've seen videos of Kay Slay and Clue beefing over the Justo Awards, back when it meant something, when it was about respect. Now a DJ will happily put out a mixtape that isn't mixed. No exclusives, no real effort.

How would you say the transition to the digital format has affected your work?

Around the time I started, DJs would put out one mixtape at a time or maximum three or four. Later all the big DJs were putting out 10 to 15 covers just to recoup the amount they were originally getting back when they were selling physical copies. These were the good days for me, monetarily. They did kind of spark the end of the actual mixtape, though. Of course, there are still DJs putting out tapes but most people will say it's not the same. I've noticed now that I get a lot more work from independent artists, which isn't a problem. Sites like LiveMixtapes, DatPiff, CrackMixtapes or FreshNew-Mixtapes have just become the store fronts now.

And the DJ has also in many ways been replaced by the likes of Evil Empire and Trap-A-Holics, who are more like publishers in a way, right?

Yeah, Evil Empire has been around since the DJs, though. It just shows that you don't have to be a DJ to do a DJ's job.

Do you have anything that you would refuse to do from a moral perspective? For example, Miami Kaos doesn't do religious imagery and stopped doing explicit stuff because of his Christian beliefs.

I have no morals. Nah, I mean, obviously there are subjects that I wouldn't do. Like anything that condones child pornography or bestiality and stuff like that, but I'm not a religious person. I always enjoy a cover where you can push boundaries. Regarding this matter, there are two covers I did for Plies a couple years ago (see above, editor's note). They brought up quite a bit of conversation and controversy because of the subjects and concepts.

Lil Wayne, The Syndicate & Digital Product
No Ceilings No Walls 2 – Most Wanted, The Get Away!

Tapemasters Inc. & Bun B
OG Bun Pt.2

Evil Empire
Grand Hustle Muscle

Waka Flocka Flame & Gucci Mane
So Icey – Entourage

The Game
America's Most Wanted 2

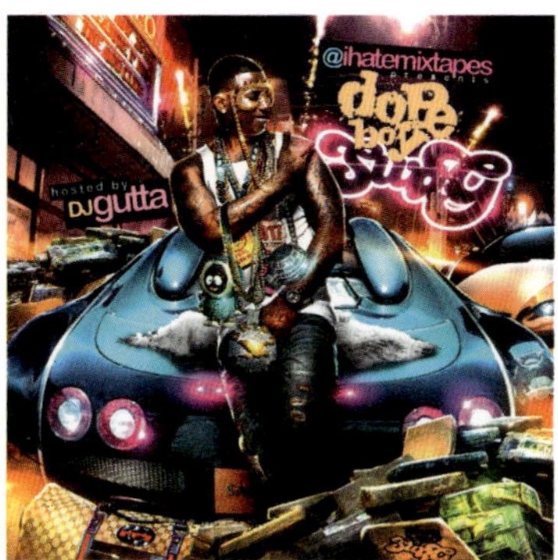

Ihatemixtapes presents
Dope Boy Swag

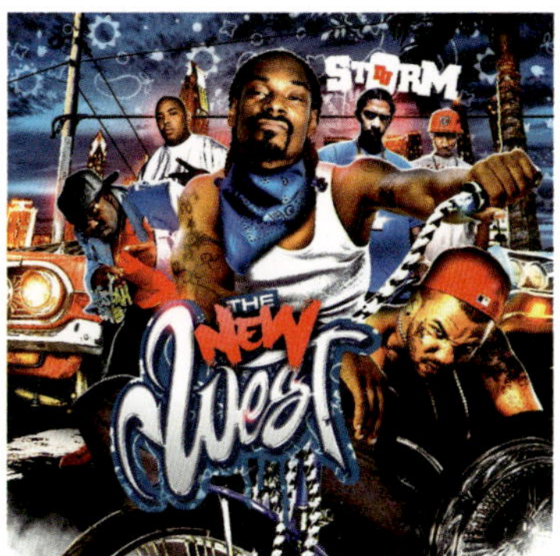

DJ Storm
The New West

Big Stack$$$ & DJ 5150
My Chain Costs More Than Your Box Chevy

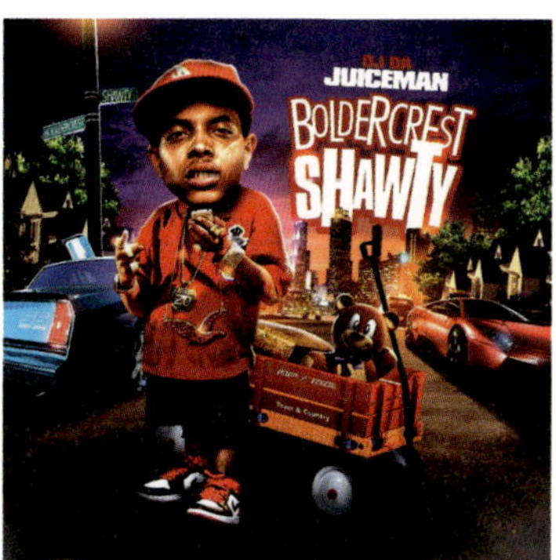

OJ Da Juiceman
Boldercrest Shawty

DJ P Exclusivez & Big Stack$$$
Stacks On Deck 2

DJ 5150 & B.G
Chopper City 2004

A-Mafia & DJ Diggz
Lord Of The Streetz

Tapemasters Inc. presents Juelz Santana & Jim Jones
Forever Harlem

DJ P Exclusivez & Zaytoven
Zay Town Vol.3

Gucci Mane & DJ Holiday
Trap Back

Byrdgang presents Mel Matrix
Red Apples Falling

OJ Da Juiceman & DJ Fletch
Juice On The Loose

DJ Prophecy
South Bound Down 4

Armstrong, DJ Holiday & D-Strong
Kold World Kold Blood

Future, A1 & FBG
Streetz Calling

Young Scooter, DJ Swamp Izzo, DJ Green Lantern & DJ Smallz – *Married To The Streets*

The Syndicate & Digital Product present Gucci Mane & Lil Wayne
The Repo Men

Pimpin' Curly & Officer Ricky
Kiss My Pinky Ring

Sound City presents
31 Flavors

Webbie
Macho Man Savage

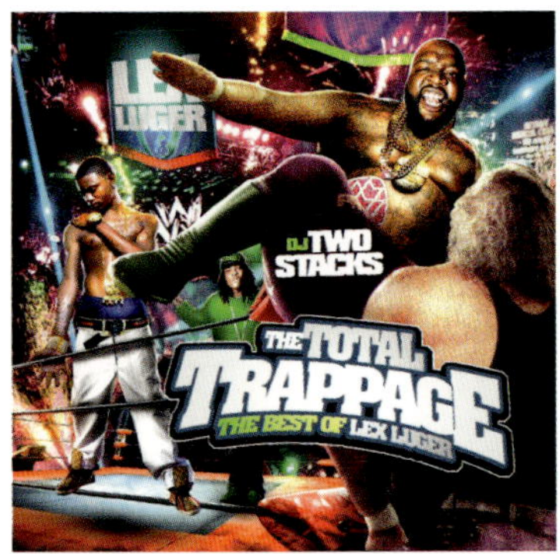

Lex Luger & DJ Two Stacks
The Total Trappage – The Best of Lex Luger

Lex Luger, DJ Two Stacks & DJ Me$$iah
The Total Trappage 2 – The Best of Lex Luger

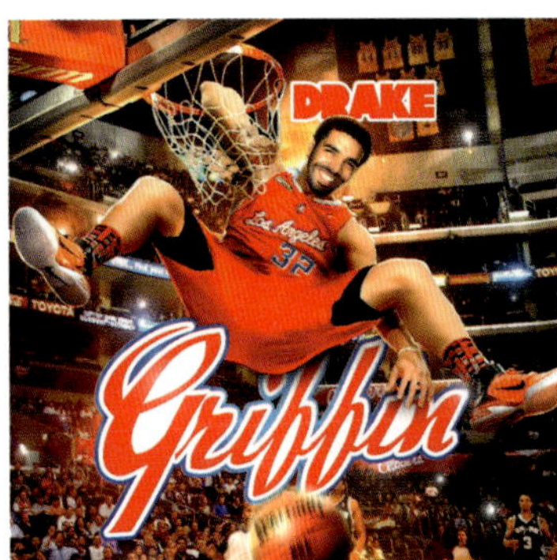

Drake
Drake Griffin

Waka Flocka & DJ Love Dinero
Duflockarant – Halftime Show

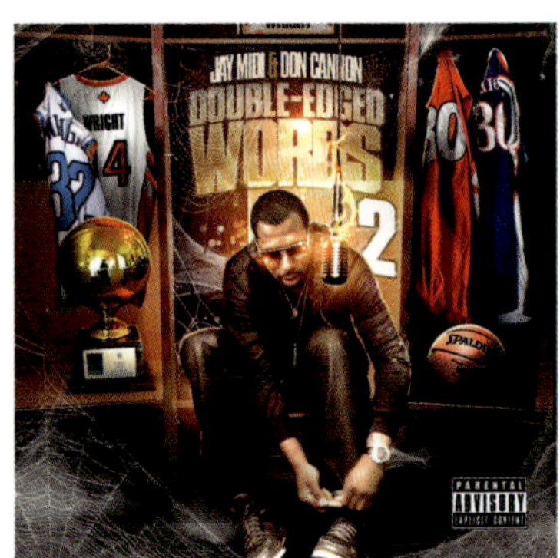

Jay Midi & Don Cannon
Double-Edged Words 2

Dr Dre & Eminem
The Sorcerer's Apprentice

The Empire presents Lil Boosie & Webbie
Swine Flu

Vado
Slime Time

Prophecy presents
DFB Deep Fried Blends 5 – ATL Edition

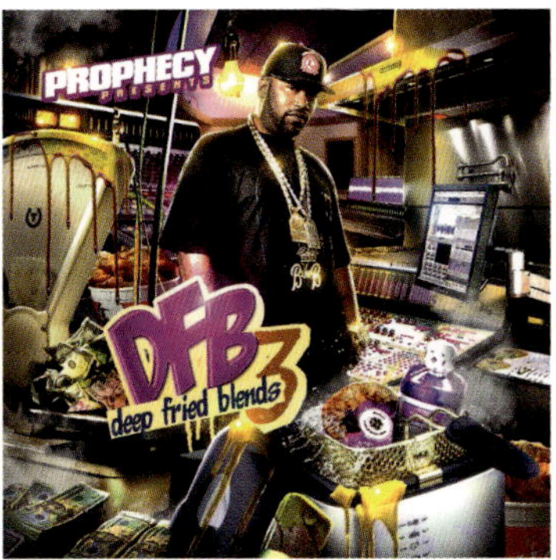

Prophecy presents
DFB Deep Fried Blends 3

Prophecy presents
DFB Deep Fried Blends 7

White Boy Swag Ent. presents Yo Gotti
5 Star Chef

DJ Fletch, T-Pain & Lil Wayne
Lil' Pain

OJ Da Juiceman & Don Cannon
Boulder Crest Day

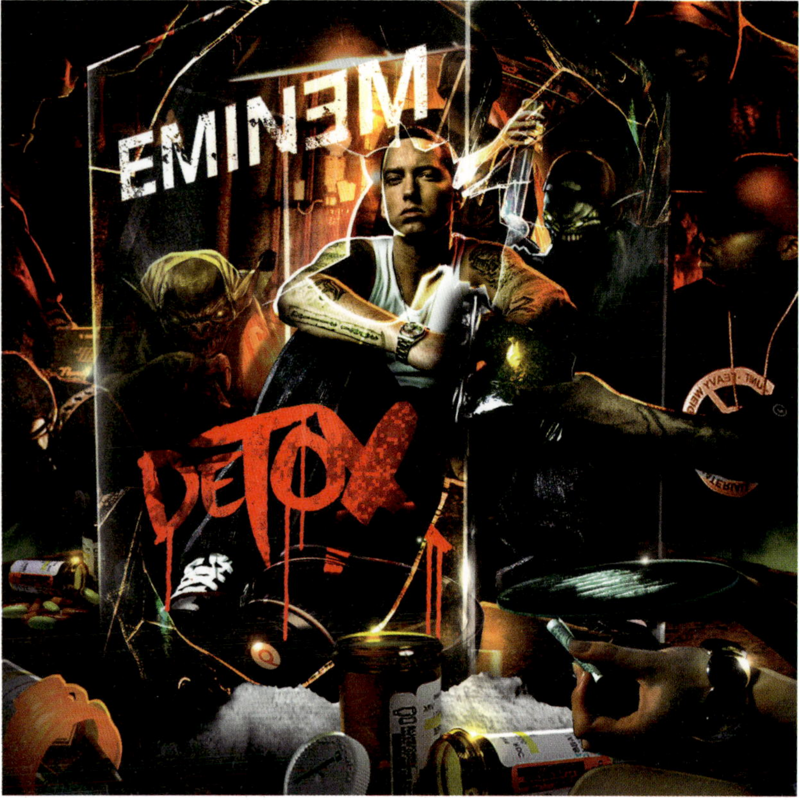

Eminem
Detox

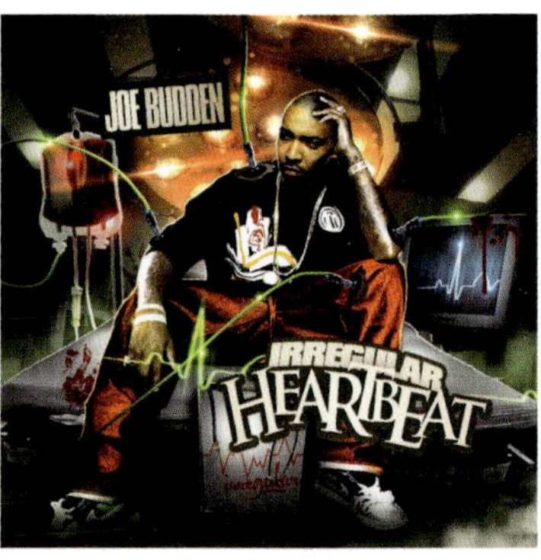

Joe Budden
Irregular Heartbeat

Lil Wayne
Tear Drop Tune Pt.3

It's surprising how rarely you see covers that really shock considered that it's such an unregulated industry.

Yeah, I guess so. But I think it's pretty hard to shock people, in general, nowadays.

If you could live one day inside the world of one of your mixtape covers, what would that day look like?

Well, I imagine there would be a lot of living to excess. A lot of money, women and firearms. Probably 10,000 miles away from my real life and probably not somewhere I would like to stay for long.

Could you pick one of your favourite covers and explain it?

At the time, I didn't know that this concept was inspired by *Game of Thrones* because I'd never seen the show. But the artist described how he wanted it to look. Ransom contacted me saying that he was about to drop his biggest tape to date, hosted by DJ Drama. It was his best music so the cover really need to make an impact. I asked if he had any ideas and he told me *The name of the CD is 'Winter's Coming' so I want the crown placed on my head has to look weathered and beaten up by the viciousness of the worst winter storm.* I replied *Yeah, I was thinking of incorporating snow and ice building up on the crown, falling off in front of your face in places, icicles and all that. It will look crazy.* He then sent me two tracks from the tape, *Insanity* and *Stand A Chance*. He sent me a couple of photos. I knew I wanted to work with a face shot rather than a full body because of the level of detail I had in mind. I started with sourcing a crown. It sounds easy but finding a high-res royalty-free image of a crown that isn't from some child's playset isn't an easy task. From there, I started working on the weathered part of the face. I wanted to make it look like an old statue made of cracked stone.
The original version had smaller part of the face covered by the stone effect because, in the past, a lot of artists don't like their faces to be edited. I built up the textures in the foreground, the rain and snow. I knew I wanted quite a subtle color way. Dusty blues and greys to reflect the dullness of winter. His skin also needed desaturation but I didn't want it to match the stone. I wanted it to remain human. The text was pretty much the last thing I tackled. I thought the graphic had a cinematic or theatrical impact. For the presentation text I opted for a font used at the bottom of movie posters. I chose the *Ironmongers* font for the artist and DJ text and an edited version of a font called *Xenippa* for *Winter's Coming*. I chose to ornament using some heraldic swooshes. The final work file was around 90 layers including adjustment layers.
The client only asked me to make two changes in total, to make the title golden and to add more cracks to the face.

Ransom & DJ Drama
Winter's Coming

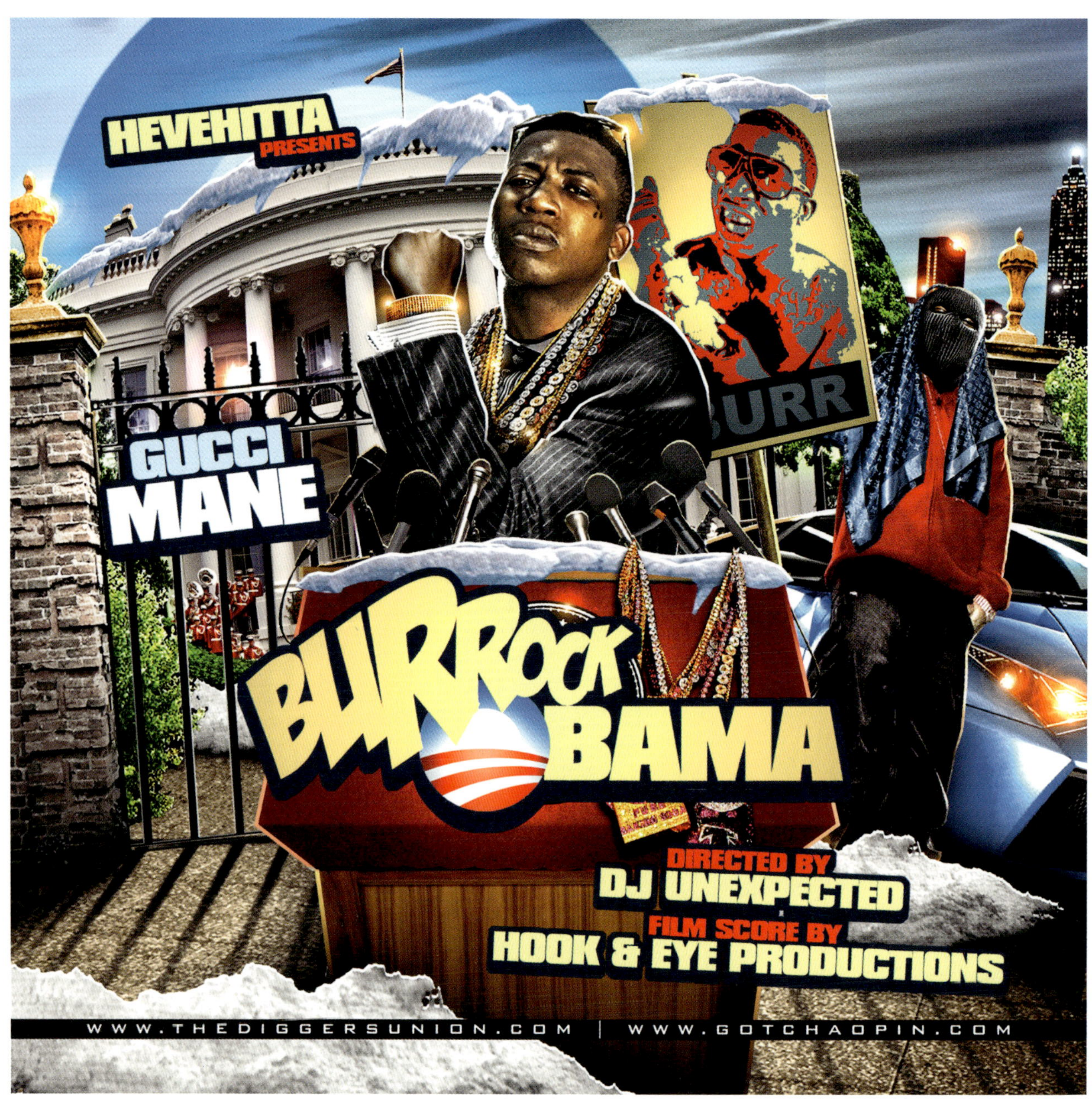

Hevehitta presents Gucci Mane
Burrock Obama

Hoodrich Entertainment presents DJ Scream & Shawty Lo
I'm Da Man Pt.3

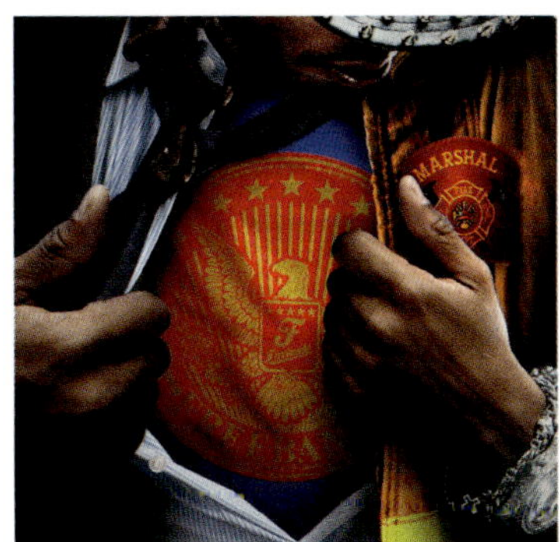

Future
Super Future

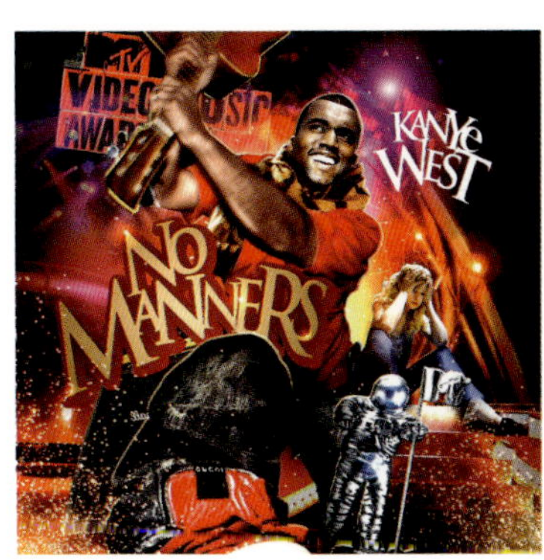

Kanye West
No Manners

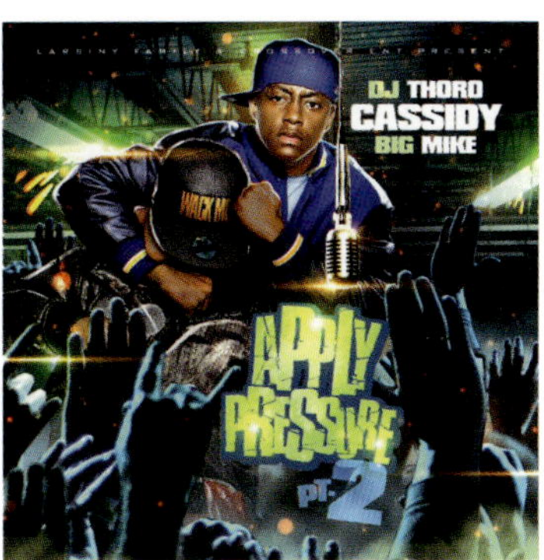

Larsiny Family & Crossover Ent present DJ Thoro, Cassidy & Big Mike – *Apply Pressure Pt.2*

DJ Diggz, DJ Lust & Big Mike present French Montana & Max B
Coke Wave – The Official Best Of

Hoodrich Ent presents DJ Scream & Jim Jones
Coke Rush

Trap-A-Holics, DJ Spinz & Cartel MGM
Kilo Lingo

The Syndicate & DJ Spinatik
Stash House 11

Yo Gotti, DJ Drama & Zedzilla
Cocaine Muzik 4 – Both Sides, Both Stories

Tapemasters Inc.
So Icey – Xmas

Yo Gotti
White America

The Syndicate, DJ Rell, Young Jeezy, Gucci Mane & T.I.
ATLiens

DJ Drama & OJ Da Juiceman
Orange

Miami Kaos

Tellemlook.com & Above All DJs present
Fetti Kings 9

Despite his name, Miami Kaos isn't from Florida, but rather born and raised in the Bronx. Growing up in the birthplace of hiphop, Miami Kaos has had a natural inclination for art for as long as he can remember. *It started with me drawing cars, Speed Racer and the Batmobile. Then I began to draw people and kind of excelled at it. When my school would have art competitions with the other districts, the principal told me, 'we need you to go. Create something!'. Most times, I won. I think I only lost once.*

Miami Kaos's creativity eventually led him to the graffiti world, where he developed his moniker. *When I was a kid, I had this toy sports car, something like a Ferrari. And I used to dress different. I didn't wear sneakers too much. I wore silk shirts and shades. So my friends used to tease me and call me 'Miami Vice.' So when I began doing graffiti, I started writing 'Miami' and I added 'Kaos' as it was a crew I was involved in.*

Miami Kaos found inspiration from other cultures not typically associated with hiphop. *I was heavily into Japanese animation, anime. Those cartoony styles really caught my eye. So when we had to do life drawings in school, I looked at it through the filter of anime. I felt like 'I don't need to know*

Eminem, DJ 2Mello, Prophecy & Miami Kaos
Avenger

this, I'm going to be a cartoonist. I don't need to know proportions and light shading because that's not where I'm going'. Miami Kaos eventually honed his skills for realism based on his appreciation of comic book art. Seeking to emulate the styles of Marvel and DC Comics illustrators such as Alex Ross, his artworks began to look more like classical paintings than cartoons. *I started using image references and really took my time to make my illustrations look realistic. When I stopped to look around, I didn't see anybody else, especially in hiphop, that was doing what I was doing.*

In the fast-paced world of mixtape cover artwork, where Photoshopped collages dominate, Miami Kaos is an anomaly for his use of more traditional methods, such as sketching by hand. *I can see a difference in the age groups because I'm born in 1979 and far into my 30s. People around my age remember the time of airbrushed t-shirts and look at my work as drawings. Younger people always assume there has to be a computer software behind everything. They can't imagine somebody actually doing this using a pencil. A pencil, this arcane tool.* Even though the end result of Miami Kaos' work is made with a computer, his ability to draw both on and off the screen have set him apart from the majority of mixtape designers who rely completely on existing images, which has

DJ Black presents
Ridin Dirty Vol.11

Drugs on Music presents DJ Lazy K & French Montana
Cocaine City Volume 12

Ace Kannon and DJ Homicide
Loose Kannon

Izzy, Crush, JR & Chillaa – So Seriuz Fam
Why So Seriuz?

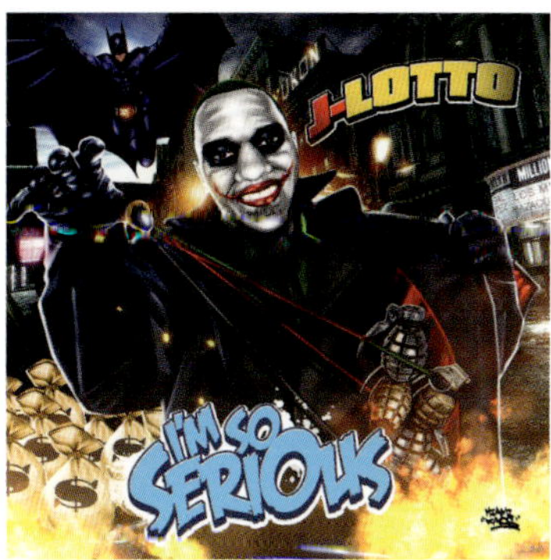

J-Lotto
I'm So Serious

Guerilla Entertainment presents DJ Kush & Taj He Spitz
Got Purp Volume 03

helped him achieve his dream of becoming the Alex Ross of hiphop.

The influence of comic books on Miami Kaos' work is apparent, as he transforms MCs and DJs into the superheroes that they often portray themselves to be in their lyrics. Perhaps this is why his work has been in such high demand. *I've always felt that if I don't go over the top, if it's not looking crazy, you might as well use a photograph of the rapper. Like, what would be the point of asking me to draw something just to draw it? Sometimes people say, 'I just want to sit and count money'. And it makes me wonder, 'why don't you just use photographs?'. I'm the dude that you come to and say 'I want to be punching through a wall, running with a bag of money like I just robbed a bank. The cops are shooting at me but the bullets just bounce off of me'.*

Miami Kaos' imaginative illustrations pull the viewer into fantastical visual interpretations of decadence, violence and extravagance often referenced in rap lyrics. While the mixtape industry is full of competing graphic designers constantly copying each other's styles, Miami Kaos' aesthetic is unmistakable and has proved impossible for other artists to replicate. *I've seen people trying to copy me. But I think that I built my brand to where people think it's better to not have work from Kaos than to have a fake Kaos. Because a fake Kaos makes it look like they can't afford the real thing. So I see very few imitators around.*

Unlike the majority of self-taught graphic designers in the mixtape industry, Kaos has benefited from a formal fine arts education where he enjoyed many supportive teachers. He recalls an exercise where a teacher gave pictures of human faces for the class to draw, but made them turn the photos upside down. *That way he taught you to draw what you actually see opposed to the mind. Sometimes you take certain liberties based on memorised images. But if it's upside down, you'll draw exactly what you see, the actual shape. It helped a lot.* Miami Kaos also received criticism from his teachers when his style had become so distinct that the whole class immediately recognized it was him. *I remember one day a teacher got mad and lectured us, or me specifically, that a designer having a specific style was wrong. You should be able to adjust for whatever type of work. I didn't see it that way. Even back then, I thought that if you have your style, that's what sets you apart from everybody else.*

After almost a decade in the industry, Miami Kaos has learned to adapt his formal art education to the chaotic culture of hiphop mixtapes. *At school, they taught you that a logo should start at 1,000 dollars. And in the mixtape industry, if you tell somebody it'll cost them 1,000 dollars, they would ask 'are you high?'. I talked to a guy the other day, he had 75 dollars to spend on a logo design. I gave him the price quote, I think I suggested 200 dollars and he was like 'that's double what I expected to pay'. And it's funny because you think you're cheapening yourself while some people think you're overpricing your work.*

Despite his life-long love of hiphop, Miami Kaos never set out to be an artist working for the music industry. *No, that stuff kind of found me,* he admits. After finishing college, he began working a clerical job for the city's sanitation department, with long-term job security and good pay. He was friends with Star, the ex-Hot 97 radio DJ from the duo Star & Buc Wild, who supported Miami Kaos' work and wanted to help him pursue his artistic dreams. *Star used to tell me, 'I don't have any money, but when I get on, I'm gonna put you on because I like what you're doing'.* One day at work, Kaos received a call from Star saying that they were flying to Los Angeles to sign a record deal and they wanted him to come make their album cover. Kaos asked his supervisor if he could take a week off but was refused. *So right then and there, I had to choose. I had safety. I had an actual city job. But I said, 'Well, I'm leaving. It is what it is'.*

The album cover for Star & Buc Wild never worked out, but things fell into place when Kaos ended up getting some work for *The Source* magazine. There he met Big Tigger, back then one of the hosts of Black Entertainment Television show *Rap City. Big Tigger has been like my big brother and mentor during all these years. He introduced me to a lot of celebrities and he got me a lot of work, with Nas and all these guys. Whenever he would meet with them, he would tell me 'so-and-so is coming through to the studio tomorrow. If you got something to show him, or if you wanna meet him and talk to him, come through'. So I would do that.* Kaos ended up in Miami for *The Source Awards*, where he was asked to design a mixtape cover for a local unnamed radio DJ.

I always say that it was God who told me 'do it', when I was offered that job. Not my ego. Because, honestly, it was about 175 dollars or something like that. If I had had a big head, I would have laughed at it because of the money I was making from other work I was getting at the time. But some of my friends talked about going out to Wet Willie's, this popular spot that everybody would go out to drink at in South Beach. So I said, 'Okay, you know what, I'm gonna do this thing for the 175 dollars and I'm going to treat everybody with that pay'. Not expecting to find work in Miami, Florida, he only had some pencils with him. In the end he spent most of the fee to rent a Kinko's booth to finish the mixtape cover.

I did the cover and sent it to the DJ on Friday or Saturday. By that Monday, I guess the mixtape was moving fast. I had put my phone number on it and within two days, my phone just started ringing off the hook. Everybody was like 'Hey, could you do a mixtape cover for me? I want a mixtape cover!'. At that point, I started taking some orders but I said that I wasn't going to be able to do it until I got back to New York. That was how I started doing mixtape covers. And from there the requests kept coming in and in and in.

Please describe your creative process.

First, I get the concept. Either somebody says *this is what I want* or sometimes you get people that say *I've seen what*

DJ 2Mello & Miami Kaos & The Labor Department
The Remix Killa

Kochece & DJ Mino presents
Do You Believe In Ghosts Part 8

DJ Trigga, 50 Cent, Jadakiss, Fabolous & Jay-Z
Fantastic 4

DJ Dub Floyd, Miami Kaos, Drake & Nicki Minaj
The Wonder Twins

Chosen Few presents Young Tef
SSX2 – Super Sayings X2

DJ Dub Floyd, Miami Kaos, Wiz Khalifa & Lil Wayne
Ringleaders

DJ Trigga
Gucci Mane vs Young Jeezy

DJ Cool Breeze presents Lil Wayne
My Own Worst Enemy Part 2

Maino & DJ Trigga
I'm The Victim

We The Best Music Group & Def Jam [illegible]
Body Bags

Dj 2Mello, Prophecy, Miami Kaos & T.I.
I Always Got Away With It Part 3

Fabolous, Young Jeezy & Saran
Dead The Funeral

Trap presents
DAG2H – Died and Gone 2 Heaven

Jay-Z, Kanye West, Drake, Lil Wayne & DJ Trigga
Watch The Throne

That Crack & DJ 2Rek
Fuck Dat Piss Edition Part 6 – Flava In Ya Ear

Bishop The Greek
Rap's Renaissance

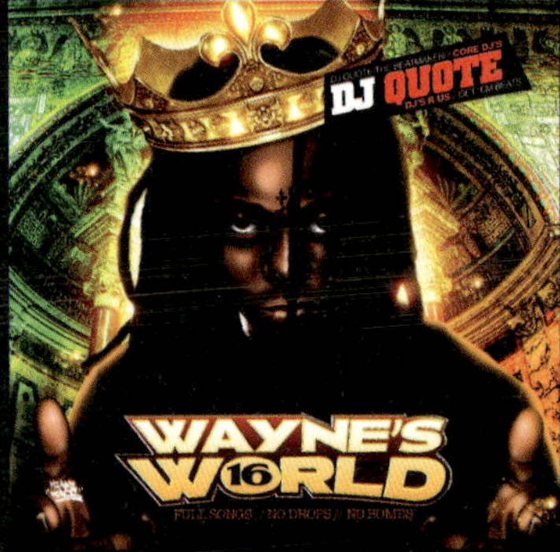

DJ Quote & Lil Wayne
Wayne's World 16

Loud Gang presents Pop Got Barz
Heir To The Throne – Welcome to New London

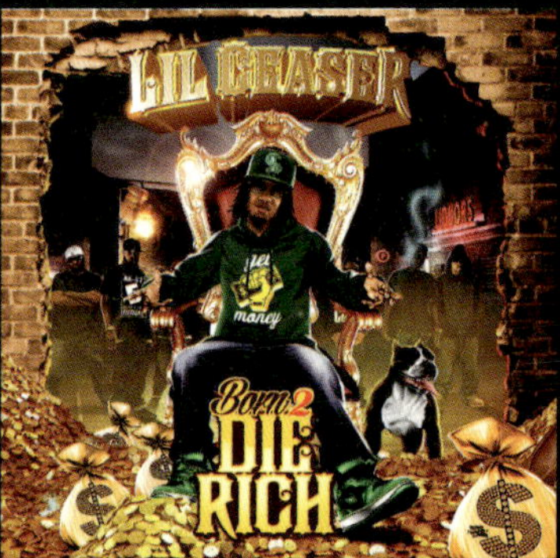

Lil Ceaser
Born 2 Die Rich

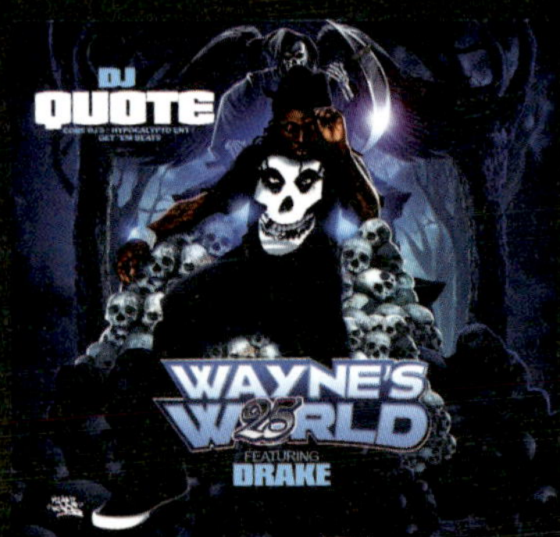

DJ Quote & Lil Wayne featuring Drake
Wayne's World 25

Lowkey
Angel Of Death

DJ Madden & Big Pun
Immortal Punishment

Yahway music presents DJ Madden & Tupac
Makaveli Returns

Dangerous Gunz presents Lil Kurt & E.X.
The Slaughtermore Project

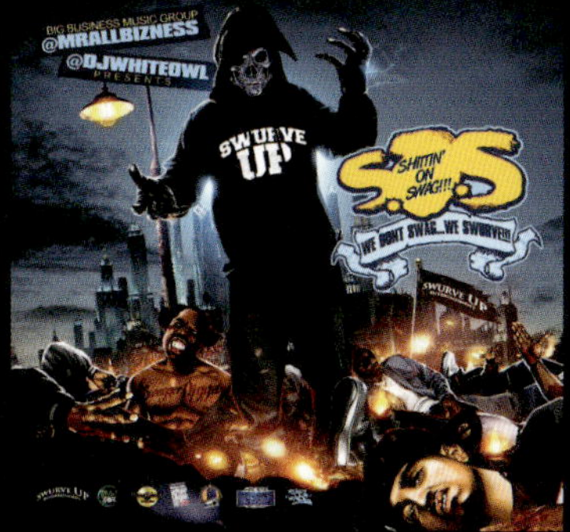

Mr All Bizness & DJ Whiteowl
S.O.S – Shittin' On Swag!!!

Lordz In Power presents
T.A.L.E.N.T.

A YNGMRadio.com presentation Future
Freeband World Order

DJ Illmatic, DJ Skullator, Tapestars & Money Mars
Destined to Reign

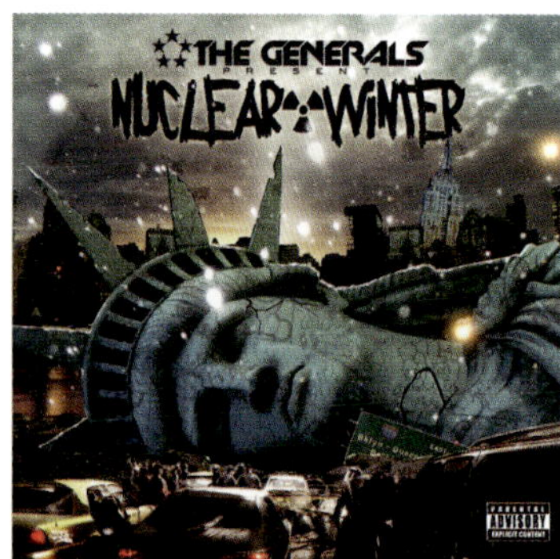

The Generals present
Nuclear Winter

DJ Whiplash & Brielle
A Christmas Star

NWEMG presents Driicky Graham
Ya Gotta Start Somewhere

you can do. This is the title of the mixtape, you do what you feel like. Even with that freedom, before I start to do actual work, I explain the idea so they agree with what I'm doing and that we're on the same page. Again, from that point on you have two different kinds of people, the ones who wants to control you and the ones who give you freedom. I'm getting the later one a bit more nowadays, but it used to be rare. But there's still people who say *I want to be kicking the door in* and they send a picture of themselves, a reference on how they look. A face shot or full body so I see their size. Then I reference stuff. I might Google *kicking the door in* or *kicking.* Sometimes I even ask one of my friends to kick and work with a reference like that and then I begin putting it all together. Sometimes clients send photos of the situation, like *this is me kicking, here's an image.* When I start drawing, I ask them *do you want to be dressed the way you're dressed or are there specific gear you want to be wearing?* Stuff like that. Then I do the sketching and I show it to them. If it's one of those projects where people don't bug me on time, then I keep them involved in the process. But the people who are rushing, saying *I need this, I really need it soon,* I just go in and do it all the way to the finish. When it's done I send them the cover and I also send them the clean art, without the text.

Even if you don't see certain elements inside the frame of the final cover, I still drew it. If you see somebody in a standing pose and you don't see their feet because of the text or something being in front of them, that doesn't mean that I didn't draw their feet.

Does it happen that you prefer the art without the text?

Yes, because the text can make or break the cover. Sometimes people have too much verbiage. *So-and-so entertainment presents... The Macchiavelli God Almighty so-and-so... starring in...* And then the title is: *Yo! Get Off My Block I'm Back For What I Deserve... Hosted by So-and-so and Whatever-Whatever.* That really kills my vibe.

When it comes to the creative process, do you prefer total freedom or do you like limitations?

I enjoy the freedom. I enjoy projects when people just say *do what you want to do, I'm in no rush.* Because that's when I get to do extra stuff. In cases like that, even if I charge a certain amount, I always give them more than what they pay for because I'm just looking at doing the best that I can with it. But there are covers where people really control me, I have had people telling how to do everything down to a pair of socks. *I want to be wearing Polo socks and I need to be wearing this kind of belt wrapped around and these pants and this shirt.*

Obama Music Foundation presents DJ Obombya
American Money

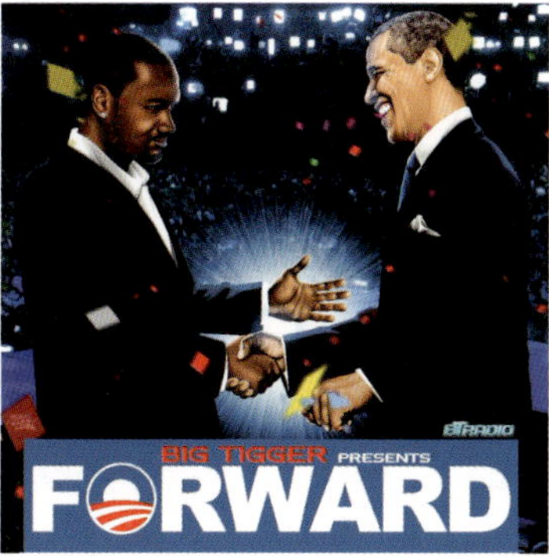

Big Tigger presents
Forward

Camiliano feat. AG Da Coroner, Mayhem Lauren & J-Love
The Reform

And I want to be standing facing this way with my hat tilted three quarters and blah-blah-blah. That's not really any fun because that's when I feel like I'm working, like an employee. And then they need it quick, too. *I need this as soon as possible. As soon as you can, just get it back to me.*

What I don't like either is when I ask somebody for their concept and they just show me a lot of my own work and they go, *I'd like something like what you did here. Do the letter that you had there.* That's no fun either because then I have to go back to stuff that I've done already, to repeat myself. That was a problem with the designers on the Slumz Boxden online forum. Some of them don't know these work situations, so when they criticize you, saying *he already used that car on that other cover*, they don't know that somebody asked to have that specific car in there.

How has the transition from physical copies to digital downloads affected your work? Are the budgets for cover art getting lower?

I don't know where it can go from here. I don't think it can ever go back to what it used to be. About the budgets, people rarely have the kind of money they used to because they're not really selling music anymore. Like with DJs doing compilations, and I'm not going to lie, they are the ones I had most fun doing because that was when somebody could just say *here's the title and the tracklist* and I could just look at the tracklist, see what's on there and do whatever I wanted to do. That was the most fun, to have that freedom. So that's why I'll prefer to work with them as opposed to someone getting really specific in their requests.

How important is the music for you when it comes to creating concepts for covers?

Not so much. If they have a really good title or single that I know of, then it might inspire, but a lot of times I draw inspiration from comic books and pop culture and things like that. So sometimes, if I know an artist and I see something in pop culture that's going on, I would put those two together. But I don't really listen to too much of the music. When I first started, during the first four years, everything that I made I got a copy of. If I did a t-shirt design, they sent me the t-shirt. If I did posters, mixtapes or albums, people would send it. Then after a while, it started to trail off. I used to listen to everything too. Every cover that I did for a mixtape or an album, if it was sent to me, I would listen to it. But it began to happen less and less after a while.

I think the most important thing to me is the artist. His personality, and from it I can usually connect to something else.

I had an idea for a cover, but we didn't do anything with it. Remember when Rick Ross got shot up and crashed his Rolls Royce and all that? I had an idea to do some *Wreck-It Ross* artwork, like the *Wreck-it Ralph* movie. In my mind, I thought that *I can draw Rick Ross in that Pixar and Disney kind of style.* I didn't do anything with that idea, but that's an example on how you would tie a concept to an artist. Another idea, again with Rick Ross, based on *The Dictator,* the Sacha Baron Cohen movie, we could have done *The Ricktator* with that big beard of his and everything. Picture Rick Ross looking like that.

I have a book, I haven't used it because of the direction that the mixtape industry started heading, but I had a concept book where I used to just write down stuff all day. As soon as I got an idea, I would just write it down. Around 2009 to 2011, I became more confident in what I was doing. If you look a lot of those mixtapes, they have my name on it, together with the DJs because I started being confident. I started getting strong ideas and DJs actually began getting at me saying *Hey, you have any ideas for a mixtape?* I would just say *give me a minute* and I would then ask one of my friends who listens to all the music *what's really hot right now?* He would tell me *this guy's hot, he's on fire.* So then I would think of a concept based on that inspiration. The beauty of that is that the clients would then pay me to do the artwork, but I never asked for them to split the mixtape money with me. I just wanted to do the artwork. So it was just like *okay I'm getting you to pay me to do something that I want to do anyway.* That was the best time.

Now you seem to be doing fewer covers, focusing on the quality rather than quantity. How many mixtape covers did you use do to every month?

At the height of everything, I think I was doing about twenty a month. Sometimes more but besides that I also designed logos, flyers and DVD covers. After a while I started saving artwork just like video game artists do. Say if I was drawing someone holding a gun, I might split it up and save the hand separately. So now if I'm in a rush and somebody needs to be holding a gun, I've got a hand holding a gun already. I started saving all my accessories. If I draw a pair of Yves Saint Laurent shades, I save that by itself now. So if I draw a picture of Nas, just his face, and want to change it quickly, I've got some shades and a Yankee hat. I put the shades and the hat on the same Nas face. So I started building my own library of elements from my covers.

How's your relationships with other graphic artists?

Now it's a little bit better than it used to be. For a while, I didn't associate with any other graphic designers because they used to tear me apart on the Slumz Boxden forum. I would say KidEight is about the only one that I'm on a friendly basis with. Illustrators, they're the ones I get along with the best because they understand my process better.

I think other designers, they used to think that I was cheating because I was doing something that they weren't doing. They used to say stuff like *if it wasn't for the illustrations, nobody would be messing with him.* But that's true. Because if I wasn't an artist, I wouldn't be a graphic designer. If I didn't know how to draw first, I would probably be doing something else.

Did you feel that it took some time for people to adjust to this new kind of illustrative style or did people embrace it from the beginning?

They gravitated to it immediately. The phrase that I used to hear a lot was *I've never seen anything like this before.* Like when I started using real photographic backgrounds and all that stuff, when your drawings and photos mix, it's hard to see what's real sometimes. What's the photo and what's the illustration. If you see my early work, I used to draw everything. But then I started using real buildings and photographies at some point, because I started getting so much work. It happened because of two reasons, I couldn't charge people the price that I would really charge to say *Okay, I'm drawing everything on this cover* and I couldn't get as much work done as I had to. But the funny thing is now I'm slowly going back to illustrating it all again, I'm taking the time because, that's how I want to evolve now. I want to do fully illustrated and painted covers.

Your earlier work was darker, with the sepia and more night-time vibes. But the color palette you're using today is a lot lighter. You've used light looking almost like a halo.

I don't know why I started doing that. I've seen other mixtape covers where people have used photos and they don't match up, so a face is kind of reddish but the hand for that person is yellow. When I made everything darker, it unified everything in the same tone. I always try to make sure that my work never looks like anybody else's. I always make sure it's different.

Are there any visual trends over the years that you have enjoyed, jumped on, or trends you tried to create?

The one thing that I wanted to do that never really went anywhere, I wanted to bring back graffiti. But it didn't really stick. I've drawn in graffiti style. I've made characters cartoony like in graffiti and that didn't really pick up. But the main thing that I really wanted to get across but didn't manage to was to introduce the superhero stuff. I was working with DJ Dub Floyd and for a while we were trying to do superhero-themed covers. We did Rick Ross as the Kingpin from Daredevil. Then we did Drake as Shazam. Stuff like that, and draw up connections between the two cultures. Drake has his smile and he's yellowish, like light-skinned. And in the comic Shazam, there is Captain Marvel, they call him the Big Red Cheese. So as Drake is light skinned he became the Big Red Cheese. I was playing around like that. That was the main thing we were trying to do, bring that comic flavour to it.

DJ Dub Floyd, Miami Kaos, 2520NYC, Ghostface Killah & Raekwon
Iron Sharpens Iron – Redux

Mannyman & DJ Eman present
Sub Zero – Fatality Muzik

Y.T.N.D.B
YUNG TRAVIS
STREET FIGHTER®
HOSTED BY
DJ MURDAMAN EXCLUSIVE
AND DJ KEN
RATING PENDING
RP
CONTENT RATED BY
ESRB
A TRICKIN&TRAPPIN - HYPE RADIO/DOWN SOUTH GUTTA MUZIK - AND GEORGIA MUDD PRESENTATION

Barry Bonds
Hit After Hit

Styles P, Jadakiss & DJ 31 Degreez
2 The Hard Way

Miami Kaos & DJ Dub Floyd
Next Men Vol. 03 – The Break Through

DJ Superstar Jay presents Deen
I Rebel

The Commission presents The Game & Young Buck
Laugh Now Cry Later Part 2

DJ Napster presents
ATL Shoot Out

DJ Dub Floyd
The Worst Of Screamixxes 3

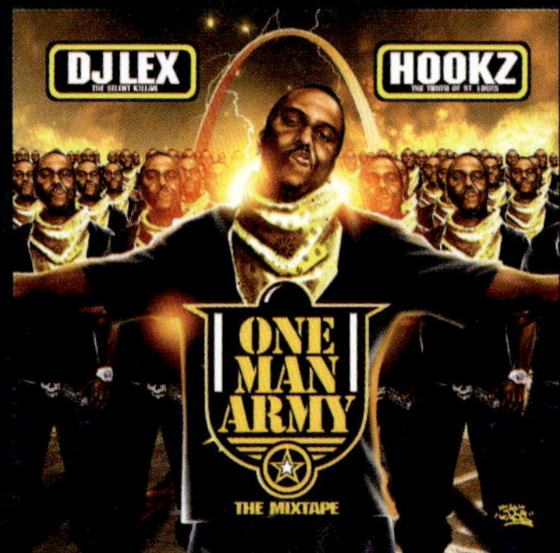

DJ Lex & Hookz
One Man Army

Jay-Z, Eminem, DJ Dub Floyd & Miami Kaos
Renegades

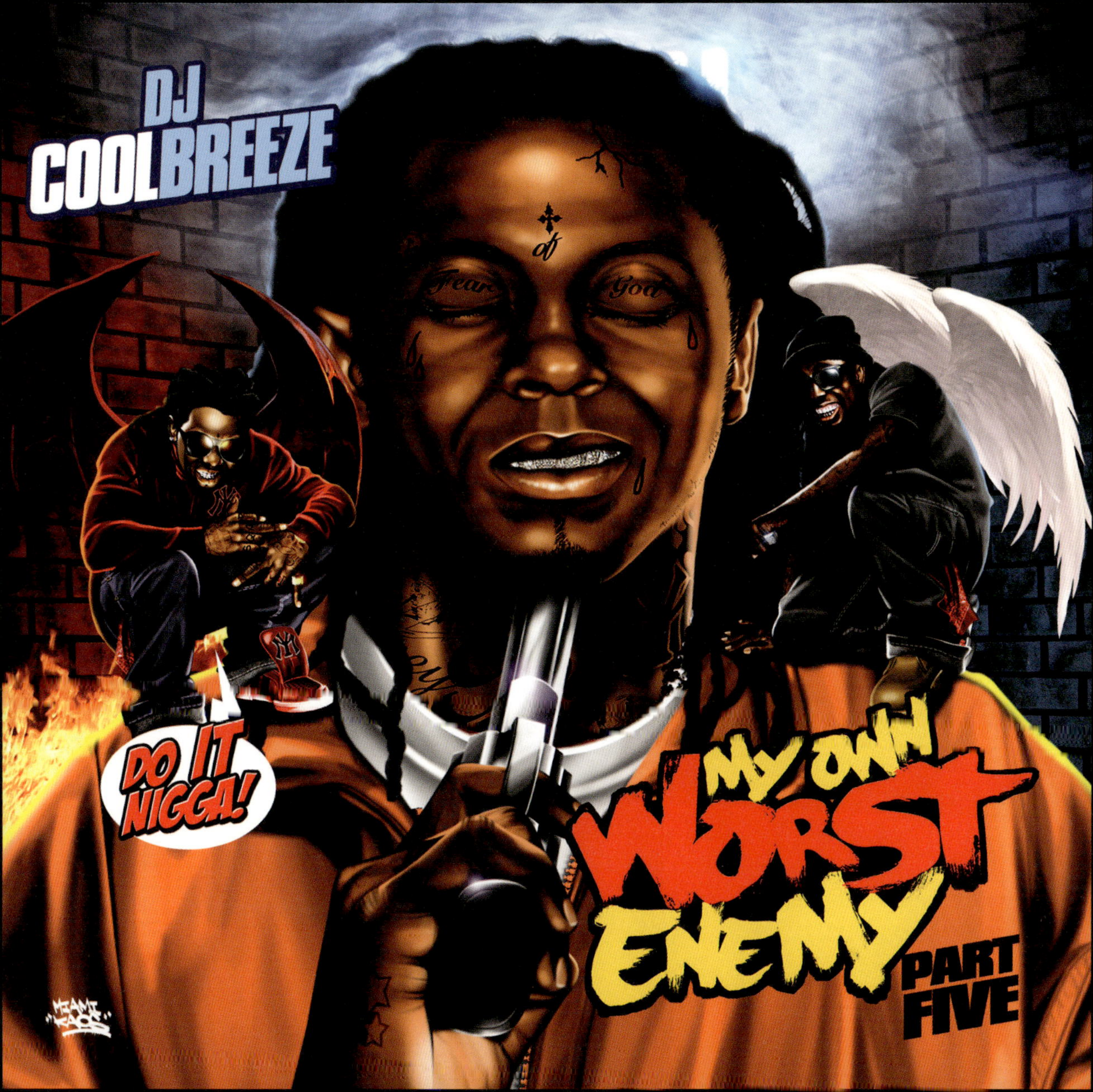

DJ Coolbreeze
My Own Worst Enemy Part Five

J. Christ
Armageddon

Bishop The Greek
Raps Renaissance Vol. 02 – Revolutionary Suicide

Kochece & D-Block
The Autopsy 2

Runt Dawg
The Best Of Runt Dawg

Breakthru Entertainment Music Group presents
Joe Deluxe – The Heart Of Harm

Snatchatape presents Stack Bundles
Tha Best of Stack Bundles Vol.02

Makin Moves & Build-A-Bird presents
Tsunami Wave Part 4 – The Soundtrack

DJ Blazita
Dominating The Game

DJ 2Mello, Prophecy, Miami Kaos, Wale, Wiz Khalifa & B.O.B – *Bad Company*

DJ Trigga
This Is 50 Part 2

DJ Madden present
The Art of Blending

Money Music Entertainment
Behind The Music

Slip N Slide DJs & DJ Tatt2 present
Anthony Hamilton vs The World

levehitta & DJ Unexpected
4/14/2009

DJ Coolbreeze & Slick Pulla
24

DJ Lazy K & French Montana
In Demand

)ceanz13 presents Flukey
'lu Season 2

AnthymOnTheTrack
The Last Soundbender

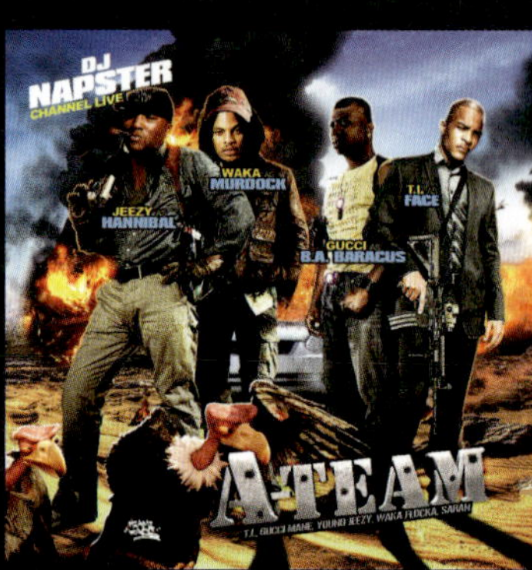

DJ Napster, T.I., Gucci Mane, Young Jeezy, Waka Flocka Flame, Saran – *A-Team*

llburn records/Pie-Rx Recordz presents A-Wax

DJ Blazita & DJ Suss One present

Highofflife.com presents Dub Floyd

Desert Storm & Bottom Lock Ent present Stack Bundles
Stack To The Future

Explosive Entertainment & Pimphop Records present
CFour – *More Than Meets The Eye*

DJ 2Mello, Prophecy & Miami Kaos featuring
Lil Kim, Nicki Minaj & Trina – *Sucker Punch*

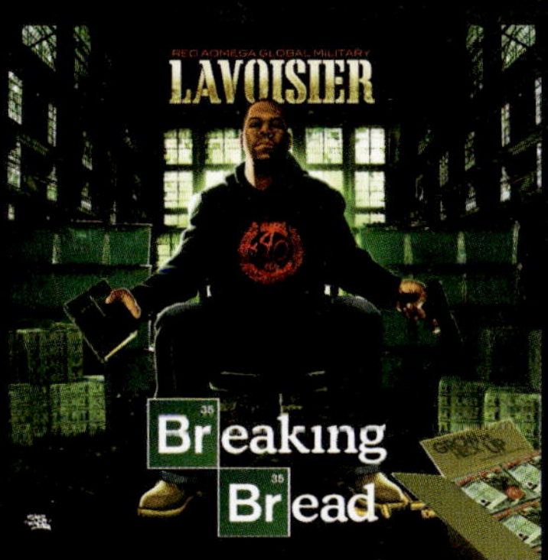

Lavoisier
Breaking Bread

Benefit
Timing Of The Godfather

J. Montana
The Crime Of The Century Vol. 01

Thirst & Shanks
Makin' Money In Recession

Snatchatape, Large Amount & A.P.
Large Paper

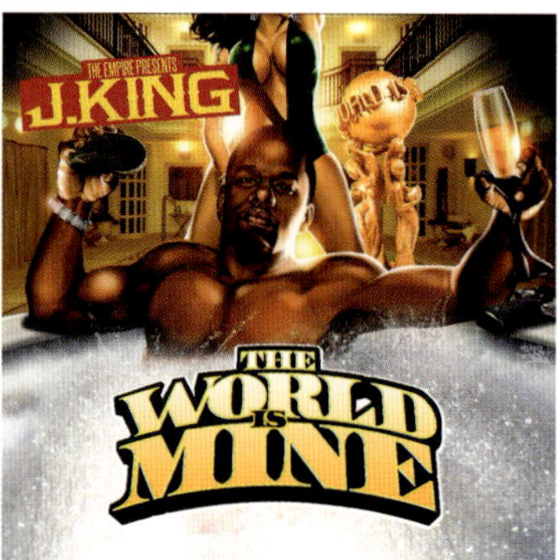

The Empire presents J.King
The World Is Mine

Lexusofficial & Worldwide Fleet DJs present
Product Of Tha Streets 77

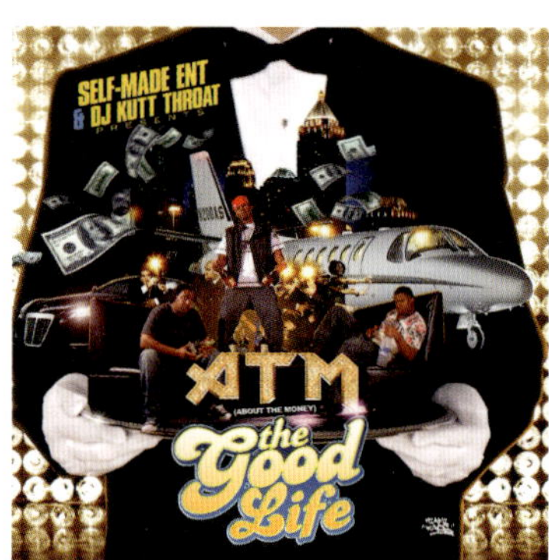

Self-Made Ent & DJ Kutt Throat presents
ATM (About The Money) – The Good Life

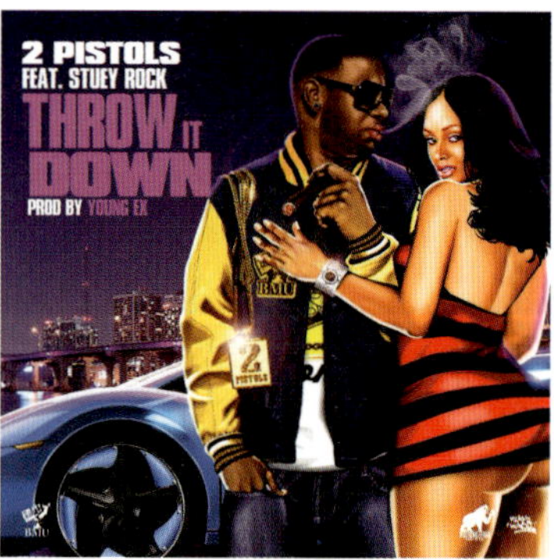

2 Pistols feat. Stuey Rock
Throw It Down

Actually I'm making another cover now as *Iron Man 3* is out. We did one last year called *Iron Sharpens Iron.* Ghostface always calls himself Tony Stark, the real name of Iron Man. On the cover, I drew Ghostface and Raekwon as Iron Man and War Machine. Now we're doing part two. That's what I really want to see, I really want to see superheroes on the covers. And I've pushed it on social media, but no one picked up on it. I've said that I wouldn't charge so much for such artwork. Because that's what I really, really want to do. If somebody would say *draw me like Captain America,* then I would do that for next to nothing because that's what I prefer to do.

Regarding visual trends in mixtapes, a few years ago mixtape covers were influenced by current events, like the 2008 presidential election or Hurricane Katrina. But more recently it seems to be changing, why do you think that is?

Because in a way, mixtapes are almost like urban news. People still want to express what's going on, culturally. This is still our medium. Either it's the actual music on, or just the designer expressing something that's going on. I think there's very few things that I've never touched on. I'm a Christian and one thing that I really don't do is religious themed covers. When people ask for a Last Supper kind of cover or to be crucified on a cross, stuff like that, I won't do it, no matter how much they pay.

But you did that Remy Ma *Shesus Christ* cover where she is depicted as crucified?

Yeah, it took a conference call of people to talk me into it. And I had a friend saying *Kaos, sometimes you've got to separate the artist from the businessman.* So in the end I agreed to do it. I think it was about a week or two later that she shot that girl. Soon after the cover came out, Nahright.com did an interview with me and they reacted to the religious theme. When the Remy Ma shooting incident happened, they hit me back and asked me a couple of follow-up questions and I said that I kind of wished I didn't do the cover. This made me stop doing interviews for a minute. Nahright made it a big thing claiming that *Miami Kaos said Remy Ma is going to hell.* And I didn't say that but they flipped it to *religious graphic artist says blah-blah-blah.* Later I did an interview for *Faded* magazine, where I said that above all else I want to *thank God… I want to thank God for this, to thank God for everything I do. I have to give Him thanks for this.* But they left out any mention of God and Christianity. I didn't like that.

You have made a lot of sexually explicit covers. Is this out of choice or is it due to client requests?

The first one I did together with DJ Digital Scale. It was the one with Eminem and Mariah Carey having sex. That's what

Digital Scale presents
Eminem vs Mariah Carey – Battle Of The Sexes

DJ 2Mello & Miami Kaos
Primeval Love 4 – Sextape Edition

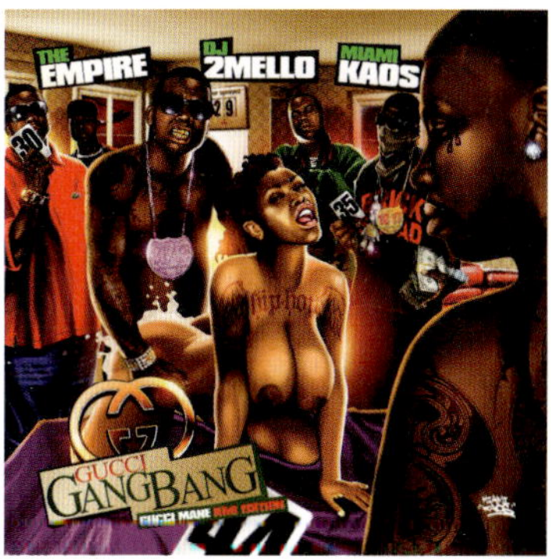

The Empire, DJ 2Mello & Miami Kaos
Gucci Gang Bang – R&B Edition

the DJ asked for. Then a couple of people started saying they wanted one. Again, as a Christian, I started feeling bad about that stuff. Because I don't look at porn, but sometimes I have to browse through sexually explicit pictures just for reference. I felt bad about that because sometimes certain people came to visit me in the studio and I had to shut down the computer or quickly close my drawing pad. But some of the CDs, especially the ones with DJ 2Mello, they were really good. Like *RnB Jamz* had some of the old R&B stuff that my mom and the older ones liked. I used to give them the CDs but I couldn't give them the covers. Those covers were winning awards though!

Is there an example of a mixtape cover where you felt like *I've gone really far with this*, far in terms of imagination?

I think some of the ones I like to call the *ultra violent*, that actually have people fighting on covers. Because I didn't like the versus style covers, where you see so-and-so versus each other but they're just standing there. So when somebody says it's a versus mixtape, I will have them literally fighting. Like the one where Rick Ross and Jeezy fight, the mixtape *Push Ya Shit Back*. I made Ross punching through Jeezy's chest and the fist goes out the back and you see Ross holding his heart.

I designed a cover that I've said I'm not ever going to show anybody. On the theme of New York versus the South. I had Jay-Z picking up Lil Wayne by his throat and Jay is simply shooting Wayne. People knowing me who saw it were like *don't show this to anybody*. I showed it to Stevie Williams, the skateboarder. He's riding with Lil Wayne and when he saw it, he said *don't let them see it, it wouldn't be good for you if they saw something like this*. So I buried that work.

Another one was for a DVD featuring Eminem. I was inspired by a photo shoot he did in XXL magazine. I had him in what looked like a trap house, shooting people. The client who I did the cover for, I didn't know he was white. And Eminem were shooting a lot of black people. So he released this DVD and I guess at first he loved it. But when we started moving with it, people started getting at him, so he came back to me. I did put a little bit of my politics in it, because I'm black. I don't really like the *N-word* and stuff like that, but I made one of the guys that Eminem was shooting wearing a shirt that said *Dead Nigga Apparel*. It was a joke amongst me and my friends, that if there would be a clothing brand called *Dead Nigga Apparel* selling 100 dollar shirts, we would buy it. So I was making fun, but I guess people started pointing it out to him. I thought he was black and would get the joke. So he came back and accused me of trying to sabotage his career. I asked *are you serious?* And he was dead serious. He thought I made this cover to hurt him, to get him beaten up. I guess he got threatened, it was crazy.

Dark Age Entertainment & Melfunk
The Shit-Uation – Funk Y'All Part 2

DJ Infamous 804, DJ King Assassin, DJ Hitman, DJ Scrill & 2 Piece
Effortless Win

DJ Rated R, Willie Maze, Crown City, Queens-hiphop.com, Doo Wop, Cormega, Miami Kaos & Big Tobacco
TE2W – Take Em 2 War Pt. 2 – The Insurgency

Team K.U.S.H. presents Blessed Trendsetta
Feed Me Rap Bitchez

Hevehitta, DJ Unexpected & Bun B
Southern Royalty

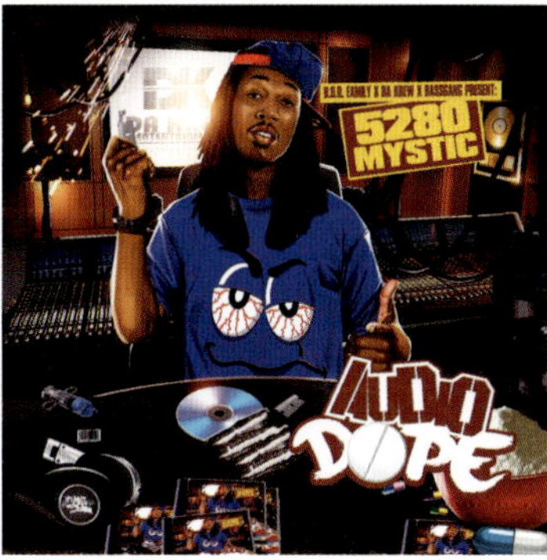

B.O.B. Family, Da Krew, Bassgang & 5280 Mystic
Audio Dope

Track Line Ent. presents E. Will
To Whom It May Concern

Sometimes your artwork is very dark, both visually and in terms of the subjects. How do you look at the US and the society? What's your view on the country and is it reflected in your artwork?

It's funny because, in the last two months, I started feeling a little bit more responsible for things. I've started thinking that maybe some of the stuff I'm doing isn't helping. But it is, on one level, separating business from the artist. If somebody would request a cover where they'll be holding an *AK-47*, I would probably say no as I'm against assault rifles. But two or three months ago, I would have done it. Even the darkest work, I would say is not from within me, it's entertainment. I watch a lot of movies and you see crazy things, it's over the top. I try to use that in my mixtape concepts. Like seeing a movie where a guy jumps from a roof and shoot ten people. I have no problem thinking it was kind of fly without personally supporting that stuff.

Visually, my work used to be different and sometimes darker. I used to put a color tone over all my work. For example *Take 'Em 2 War Pt. 2: The Insurgency.* That cover is kind of sepia and brownish tones everywhere. I stopped that around 2007 and started using natural colours. If you see anything like that where all the colours are greenish or blueish, if it has a certain hue to it, it's from before 2007.

If you could live one day inside the world of one of your mixtape covers, what would it look like?

It would be one of the graffiti ones, just because it's a safer environment than most of my mixtape covers. And that world is more colourful. Some of the covers I've done, like the ones with all the arrows. I would love to actually see that in real life, it would probably blow my mind. If I was in that world, that would be cool. And that's because I used to be a graffiti artist and I can really relate to that world a lot. I would really like bring myself to such a space.

That's a very abstract day. A day full of colours.

Too abstract? That's something I've never been able to touch on in my work. Something else is propaganda art. Like what that guy Shepard Fairey does. I like his work and some of it I get inspired by. There's times where I've tried to do stuff like that, and people say n*ah, I don't like that.* But there's only been a few times where I've tried to do work in that direction. There was a period when I used to draw more personal work. You know how they say *be careful what you wish for.* Well I remember at one point saying *I want to be so busy with paid work that I don't have time to do my personal work.* It's funny because that's where I'm at now. But to get to where I probably need to be going now, I need to do my own stuff. I'm caught on this wheel that I might have to jump off from. But there's a little bit of conflict with my ego whether I should jump off or not, a part of me don't want to jump off, or is scared to jump off.

Can you choose a cover and explain it in detail?

I'll go with the Ross vs Jeezy cover, *Push Ya Shit Back.* This was one of those where the clients asked me for a concept. At the time, Rick Ross and Young Jeezy were beefing. Rick Ross's album got pushed back and Jeezy was going at him about that. The clients, DJ Chuck T and Wiz Hoffa were saying they wanted to do a Ross vs Jeezy tape. So I came up with the title, because that's what really happened, Ross pushed his album back. If they would have had a part two, I would have had Jeezy winning. That's how I balance it, one guy is winning one time, the other guy is winning the next time. But we were just doing part one and I have a relationship with Ross more than Jeezy. I've never really worked with Jeezy. I've worked with his people, but I've done work with Ross and spoke with him personally. From there it's just a matter of you asking the client, *how far do you want to go?* The DJ might have a relationship with somebody and don't want to get in trouble. But they said that they didn't care. And actually making the artwork was easy. The only thing I had to do was to look for a reference of what a heart looks like. The rest was all about imagination and I take certain liberties. I don't care if the blood doesn't splatter realistically and stuff like that.

I looked at some references for both of the artists. I looked at a profile picture of Rick Ross, how he looks from the side. The tattoos, when I first started making tattoos, I had to find references. Especially in the 50 Cent days, back when 50 Cent was on almost every mixtape cover. I actually drew all 50's tattoos and I saved them as a file, just so when I did another 50 Cent cover, all I have to do is slap the tattoos on him. I do it like that for some rappers, it depends on who it's for. If it's for the artist himself, if let's say Rick Ross asks *draw a picture of me with my shirt off.* Then I would have to recreate all his tattoos. But for this cover I figured the average person looking at it isn't going to match it up or really scrutinize it. So I just slapped on some line work I had from before and made it look like Ross's tattoos.

DJ Chuck T & Wiz Hoffa
Push Ya Shit Back! – Def Jam Divided

Mike Rev

Tity Boi aka 2 Chainz
Southside Music

YMCMB
We Da Bizness

YMCMB
The Last Family

While growing up in Harlem and Brooklyn, Mike Rev found his way to mixtapes while exploring different forms of graphic design within the hiphop industry before the mixtape explosion of the mid 00s. *I started at a youth program called Art Start, they provided classes and workshops for teenagers that were interested in graphic design, film work, or who wanted to get into the music industry. They were pretty much a vessel to help kids learn the things they wanted to learn and connect them with different companies so they could do internships and what not.* Located on west side Manhattan, the non-profit organization Art Start provided Mike Rev with a class called Media Works. There he learned a few basics in Adobe Photoshop before the classes were closed down. *Even though they basically shut the doors, I was able to stay in touch with an instructor, asking a few questions about things I didn't know yet.* At the time, Mike Rev started doing video work for a hiphop DVD-magazine publishing company. There he also tried his hand at creating DVD covers and his design work caught the eye of some of the artists being featured in the DVD. Subsequently rappers began to request mixtape cover designs from Mike Rev. *I started hooking up with people and it just became word of mouth from there. I really never saw myself doing graphics for mixtapes. It just sort of happened.*

Mike Rev's early artistic influences are similar to many of his fellow mixtape designers. *What got me into being creative was comic books. That's what really grabbed my attention. I started drawing comic book characters like Wolverine, Captain America, and Iron Man. I loved drawing The Hulk, because of the definition of detail with the muscles. Soon after I got out of that phase, I got into graffiti, which appealed to me for the same reason. I was into the intricacy, the detail. I think that's what eventually drove me into looking at movie posters, a big influence for me.* His attention to detail is one of the factors that has made Mike Rev so successful as a designer. He never seem satisfied with his own work and is always searching for even the smallest ways to improve an image. *There's been very few projects where I've felt that they're completely done. If it isn't a matter of trying to add something extra to it, it might be something that I would like to remove or change. When I see my covers online, I catch myself thinking about the way that I could've made it better. It's been only a few times where I could honestly say that I felt a cover was complete, that there was nothing more I could do to it.*

As a perfectionist, Mike Rev can also be adamant about executing his vision for a project. *It's like when you get a song stuck in your head and can't get it out. That's usually what happens to me with a design. If I've got a clear idea, I usually roll with it. Even if the client tells me to try another concept, a lot of times I find myself still stuck with the original idea. Sometimes I have to tell the client 'this may not be the*

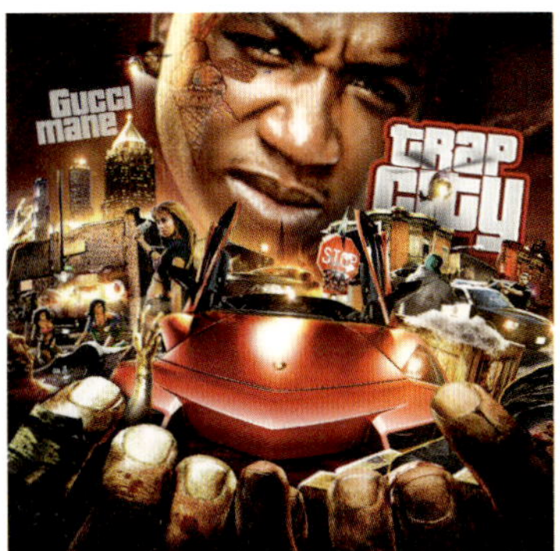

Gucci Mane
Trap City

Young Jeezy
Young & Thuggin

DJ Soulless & Bo Deal
Deal Or No Deal

Gucci Mane
My Reality

DJ Storm presents
Drank Epidemic – I Don't Need No Host 24

DJ Dephtone & Tone Trump
The Product Of Philly

direction you prefer, but if you allow me to finish the design I think you might be happy with it'. And most of the times they've been satisfied. That have meant that clients that used to try to control the direction have come back to me saying 'since that design you did was so good, I'll leave it up to you.' I've been able to convert people into trusting me. Mike Rev's commitment to his designs has led him to develop strong professional bond with even some of the biggest rappers, such as frequent client Rick Ross. *He was the first person that actually trusted my opinion about designs. Even if he had an idea, the way he would explain it was 'I trust your judgment. Do what you want. Freestyle it. Most likely, it's going to come out on fire'. So I love working with him. I also appreciate that he always hits me up early to give me enough time to come up with something creative. There's been a few incidents where I might not have delivered what Rick needed, but he'll say 'give it another shot. Maybe go this direction, but do what you got to do'. And that's the thing I appreciate most about him.*

But while Mike Rev's designs have put him in a respectable position in the mixtape world, he still sees ways to improve his career. *Sooner or later you have to ask yourself 'where do I go from here?'. I reached that point a few years ago, feeling that it's time for me to do something different. From 2006 to 2010, I did nothing but mixtape covers. A lot of the work that I'm very proud of came from that time period. But because of the direction that mixtape designs are heading, what people want on their covers, I had to say to myself 'I can't keep doing this forever, so what's the next thing?'. Maybe I should just do movie posters. Maybe I should go to school. I never went to school besides Art Start, I was never professionally taught. But then I ask myself 'is that what I really enjoy?'. That's the way I've always felt about graphic design, that it's something that I like doing. But I also really enjoyed making videos. I really did enjoy putting things together, editing clips. In reality, that was my first love. And still to this day it is my first love. So I decided to take that up again.*

Though his mixtape design work may have led him away from his first love, Mike Rev has always maintained his cinematic vision. Instead of simply repurposing existing movie posters, like many designers do, he has always approached his work with the eyes of a film director and tried to make his covers *feel like movies.* But now that he's mastered the art of the mixtape cover, he feels the need to expand his creativity beyond their 1500x1500 pixel boundaries. *If you look at some of my designs, I made it as if I was the cameraman. Like I was there and this is the way I'm filming it. That's what made me draw myself back into video work. As a director, you're able to have an imagination and make your creation come to life. When you're working on a mixtape design for somebody, you may have a vision but it might be so elaborate that you can't really fit it onto the cover. With video it's all about the complexity of my vision.*

Drake
Young Sweet Jones 3

DJ Holiday
Holiday Season 4

Meek Mill
American Dreamer

Mike Rev isn't determined to completely abandon his career in mixtape design, but simply strives to try new things and push his creativity into new areas. *I had a mentor that told me 'as long as you're doing something creative, then you're still on the right path for yourself'. Even if I'm just doing graphic design or if I started painting, as long as I stay creative, that's what I always try to keep in the back of my mind. Right now, I'm still doing graphic design, but I'm putting more emphasis into stepping my game up beyond mixtape covers.*

Mike Rev makes it clear that his top priority is his personal creative ambitions and he isn't making any promises to stick with his mixtape designs just because they're in demand. *I'm growing tired of the expectations of my designs. There's not much interest for me now. I've lost a little bit of that passion and that's when I know that I need to make a change. Don't be surprised if within a year, you don't see no more Mike Rev covers.*

Regarding your creative process, when you have a vision for a cover, does it usually hit you immediately or do you slowly find it?

I guess it's quite spontaneous. It's very hard for me to describe. Honestly, the ideas kind of hits me. Or I might see something and go *I like the way that looks, maybe I should try something with that.* You find those sorts of influences from what you're interested in. For me, a lot of it was movie posters. If I saw a poster and liked the direction it was going, I would turn it my way. You see that a lot of designers that take from the movies or advertisements or things like that. They could take something like *Got Milk?* and change it into *Got Trap?* Or they'll see a logo for a large corporation and change it to theirs.

Any movie posters you found especially inspiring?

I've seen a few movie posters that really grabbed my attention. I have two of them hanging up in my apartment. One is *Cloverfield*, the one with the torn Statue of Liberty. The second one is *Scarface*, the black and white design with him wearing the white suit. Those types of designs are so epic and that's the driving force for why people go out to the movies. Why they want to go see the movie even if they don't know if it's any good. The idea that the cover art can grab the attention like that. That's the reason that I always try to push myself when I do covers. Whether I'm doing a project for a nobody who's trying to get his name out there or somebody already established, I realised that number one thing that they want is for the cover to stand out and catch people's attention, whether people are interested in that person's music or not. When they see the cover, they will go for it and listen to the music. But at the same time, I've always given my designs a hiphop vibe. I've done projects for other types of genres but I've always maintained that I want the cover to have some kind of edge. Something that was urban, something that stood out, that represent hiphop, no matter what. That's the thing I've always kept in my mind even to this day.

Did you see these characteristics when you were growing up, back when mixtapes were being sold on the streets?

Growing up in Harlem and Brooklyn, there were plenty of places, from the bootleggers to the barber shops to the music stands, where people had their mixtapes out there and it was like a show. *I see two 50 Cent covers. One looks hot so maybe it has better music, so I'll pick that one up.* That was part of the competition back then. DJs, whether they were established or up-and-coming, really had to get the best design. The design had to be top notch. That's when I first started to realize I couldn't do design any other way. I knew that you need to make sure that the artist's picture stands out on a cover. I was at the point where I wanted to design more like movie posters, with the symbolism of them. Like *Cloverfield*, you didn't see the monster in the poster. All you saw was the damaged Statue of Liberty. That's the attraction of movie posters, you don't see the monster but you know that there's a monster in there. That's how I wanted to do album covers initially. I wanted them to maybe be without the artist's picture on it. But a lot of artists, especially independent ones, need to show their face in order to get it out there. Same thing with these DJs. If they have a cover with 50 Cent or Fabolous or Rick Ross or Gucci Mane, they've got to put their picture on it. If you don't see the artist's picture, you're going to walk by it. That's how I started to realize that I couldn't get all artsy with it. Maybe I've got to be more like the other mixtape designers. So even though I wanted to have more of a cinematic style, I did have parameters. I think any designer would say that they have parameters that they have to stay in.

Have you noticed that rappers are starting to become more open-minded to different styles of design? Perhaps simpler or more symbolic covers?

People are losing interest in those type of grand-scale designs. I've found more interest in trying to make mixtapes look like album covers. I call it the *Marshall Mathers Syndrome*. If you remember the *Marshall Mathers LP*, the cover has Eminem sitting in front of an old rickety house and it's kind of beige. It was real simplistic. I think that's the way that the market is going. These artists are trying to make it look simple like an album cover. Something more sophisticated. When I did DJ Khaled's cover for *Kiss The Ring*, I sat down with him and I thought that he wanted something grand, something really epic. But he said *all I want is my picture and just type in DJ Khaled and 'Kiss The Ring'.* That was it. I think we were done in five or ten minutes.

So is the classic mixtape cover, using the collage technique, on it's way out?

I believe so. Because with the artists that I was typically doing covers for, like Gucci Mane, that became the trend. When I was doing Gucci Mane covers, they were really vibrant and colourful, they really stood out. But what I've seen recently from him, it definitely doesn't look like the work of a freelance designer. It's more like something a record label would do. It looks real simple. I saw the cover for *Trap House 3* and it's just a picture of him and the title without much detail or definition to make it stick out. The typical artist used to always want something vibrant that stood out, very colourful and lots of stuff going on. And that isn't the case from what I've been seeing lately. A lot more covers look like album artwork. Clients will just give me a picture and want me to add a title.

Do you see this change in style as a threat to your work?

No, because I've always tried to stay versatile as a designer and not stick with one particular style. There have been times where I have done designs that are very elaborate and busy with so much going on. Then there's times when I've done designs that were rather simple. And sometimes it's been me who decided to keep it simple, not the client. Based on the concept he says to me or based of what I think of his music, I've decided that it should be simple. Maybe just a picture of his face and not so much going on. And that's because I decided that I've got to be versatile. I can't be just one-dimensional. There are a lot designers out there that just do one thing. Your niche is your niche, but you have to know that there's clients out there that might need something else.

Have you felt the shift to more simplistic designs has lowered the demand for professional graphic designers?

I think it's more about the business side than the creative. A lot of times, especially for mixtape DJs, they seem to know that music is going to sell itself. As long as the artist's picture is on there, they will be able to get those CDs to move. That's another aspect of people wanting to do more simple covers. I've noticed that some DJs that used to put out a bunch of mixtapes where every design was creative, now they're putting out the same amount of tapes but they all look the same. There's nothing creative about them. But it's because they decided that they're not going to waste time or money to invest in things like a creative cover if they know that they can move the same amount without it. The DJs are saying, *I'm not putting that type of energy into a cover, it will move on it's own.* So they can get an up-and-coming designer to do something basic and he might even give it to them for free. Just put something together and that's basically it. I understand why, because there are very few designers out there, including me, that like to take our time with our designs. I've been in situations where I've taken longer than the client wanted to. The way that I've explained it in the past is that if

Street Info presents Young Jeezy
Forever Snow

Yo Gotti
Gramlife

A$AP Rocky
Live On Lenox

The Empire & Shoot 5 Ent. presents
ATL 11

2 Chainz
B3yond B3lief

you want something top notch, I'm going to need some time. And that's something that every other designer has fought with. So if somebody else is able to take a few images and just place them together without really cleaning it up and just type in the title, and the client is comfortable with that, then that's what it is. I've even heard of some DJs picking up on design themselves. That's how far they're going to cut costs. They focus more on just getting the music out there. When I think about it, I don't blame them. At the end of the day, a lot of it is just business.

I think it also has to do with the lack of competition. A few years ago, when there were tons and tons of mixtape DJs out there, there was so much competition that they did make an effort to make sure that their cover stood out. Whether they were known or not known. Nowadays, a lot of DJs have moved on. Quite a few DJs that I've worked with in the past are doing other things. You're getting old, so eventually it's time for you to move on. So the business just isn't the way it was before.

How have these changes personally affected your work?

Well, it's one of the reasons why I've recently pushed myself to work with record labels because they pay better and they give you the opportunity to spend more time to work on designs.

Have you found it difficult to make that crossover?

It definitely is. I've found that when I reach out to certain companies or labels and show them my work, as the majority of my work looks like mixtapes, a lot of them say: *this looks fine and dandy, but it's not the direction we're trying to go.* And they maybe want to go for someone more involved with typography or something more abstract. That's why I've always had that need to be as versatile as possible. There have been certain people that believed in me enough to trust that I could be really creative with my other styles of design, like with album covers, promotional items, or posters. Sometimes work for their websites. There are a lot of programmers and web masters out there that aren't creative, and a lot of them had to reach out to me for certain designs like headers, background, and banners. So there is a group of people that still appreciate my covers, but mixtapes did pigeonhole me a little bit.

So how have things changed for you overall since you first started with mixtapes?

When I first started, I was doing it in my mom's house in front of my G4 PowerBook. It was my first year of college and I bought it from some guy. It was beat down. And look at me now, I'm married, I'm expecting a child and I have my own place. This is a complete different position to be in. A lot has changed for me. I remember back then, I didn't have to worry about a thing, so whatever money I was getting was going to clothes and technology. I have much more responsibility now, so that's another reason that I've tried to work with other things beyond mixtapes.

With the way that the market has changed, is there more demand for video work as opposed to mixtapes?

Yes, there's a huge demand for video work. And that was something that I've been thinking about. Just like how I tapped into the graphic design, I know that I can tap into the video market, too. The video industry is definitely crowded but I figure that if I can find some sort of niche, like I did with my designs, I can break through.

You discussed how you always feel like you can improve your covers. Do you have an example of when you felt a cover was fully complete?

Probably when I did *Dreamchasers 2*. That situation was kind of funny because there they, the clients, wanted to make so many changes. That was a project were I was dealing directly with the record label and they had so many requests. Things that they wanted to add, things that they wanted to take away. When you're dealing with a client like that you get to a point when you're like *this is done, this is it. I've added as much as I can add to it. I've made as many edits as I can.* And to be honest, that was a cover that I was satisfied with. The artist was very happy with the design and I appreciated that fact. That was another aspect of it, it was their project. If clients have a specific direction or specific concept in mind, I will try my best to capture that. And that was the situation with *Dreamchasers 2*. Eventually I was able to pull it off, and we both felt that eventually it was done in a good way.

You talked about the relationship you have with Rick Ross. Are there any other clients who put the same kind of trust in you?

I still come across those DJs or artists that say *I trust your judgement*. Like I said, I've been doing this for a long time, so they see the artwork, they see the track record. They know that the design is going to be hot. The question is, is it going to represent what they're looking to promote? I always aspire to try and make that happen, to capture the idea that they may have had. I remember when I did the cover for Jeezy's *Trap or Die 2*. He just told me that he wanted something that had to do with *By Any Means Necessary*. It was as simple as that, so I dressed him up in the Malcolm X outfit, and that was what he wanted.

With the most recent project I did for Rick Ross, he had put out a simple freestyle mixtape called *The Black Bar Mitzvah*. All he said was *I just want something simple*. So I took the Star of David and made it gold. It wasn't really grabbing my attention yet, but I sent it out to him early because he wanted to see something and he said *that's perfect*. And I said *well, I still want to add more to this design*. But he said no. And I appreciate that. Other times, he's given me the time to really think it through, to really come up with something that was very creative and clever. Like *Rich Forever*, and before that, the *Ashes to Ashes* cover, which was the first cover I did for him. Those were the covers that I really did enjoy doing because he gave me enough time to work on it.

Have there been instances where they've asked you to come up with the entire concept of the tape?

Yes, there's been plenty of times. Most recently, I did that for Lil Wayne. He believed in my ability to come up with something. He still has the passion for his designs to be creative. But he really don't care about the title. If it's Wayne, it's Wayne. His focus isn't on the actual title of the project, his focus is on the design. So if he wants me to come up with a title, I'll throw a title on there. As long as the design stands out, that's all that matters. So they were putting out a compilation with all YMCMB artists for Cash Money. He didn't have a name for it, he just wanted to put YMCMB on it. I had an idea to get all the artists together and then thought *let's make it look like the last supper*. Since there aren't any major rap crews around no more, like on the level that Roc-A-Fella or Dipset used to be. I decided to turn *The Last Supper* into *The Last Family*.

Do you feel the same joy working with independent artists as you do with the more established rappers?

I've been doing this for a long time. I'm going on maybe seven years now. And now, I'm not as busy as I was a year ago because it can become overwhelming when it comes to independent artists. A lot of them see some of the artist covers I do for Rick Ross or Fabolous, and they say *I need something exactly like that*. Even though their project has nothing to do with what Rick Ross did. So I made it really clear when people hit me up about designs that I wasn't really doing that much anymore. I kind of had to push it to the side because it started to become overwhelming.

It's clear that you pay strong attention to things like colours, highlights, and shadows. Can you explain how you approach those elements of your work?

It's really about making it look realistic. You get a lot of photographs where they have the light on the subject from a specific angle and I have to consider that to make the image as visually realistic as possible. My initial idea might be to do something bluish or greenish, but then I have to work with a red to make it all go together. I don't think of it like, how am I going to do the colour? How am I going to arrange the

Maybach Music Group presents Rick Ross
Ashes to Ashes

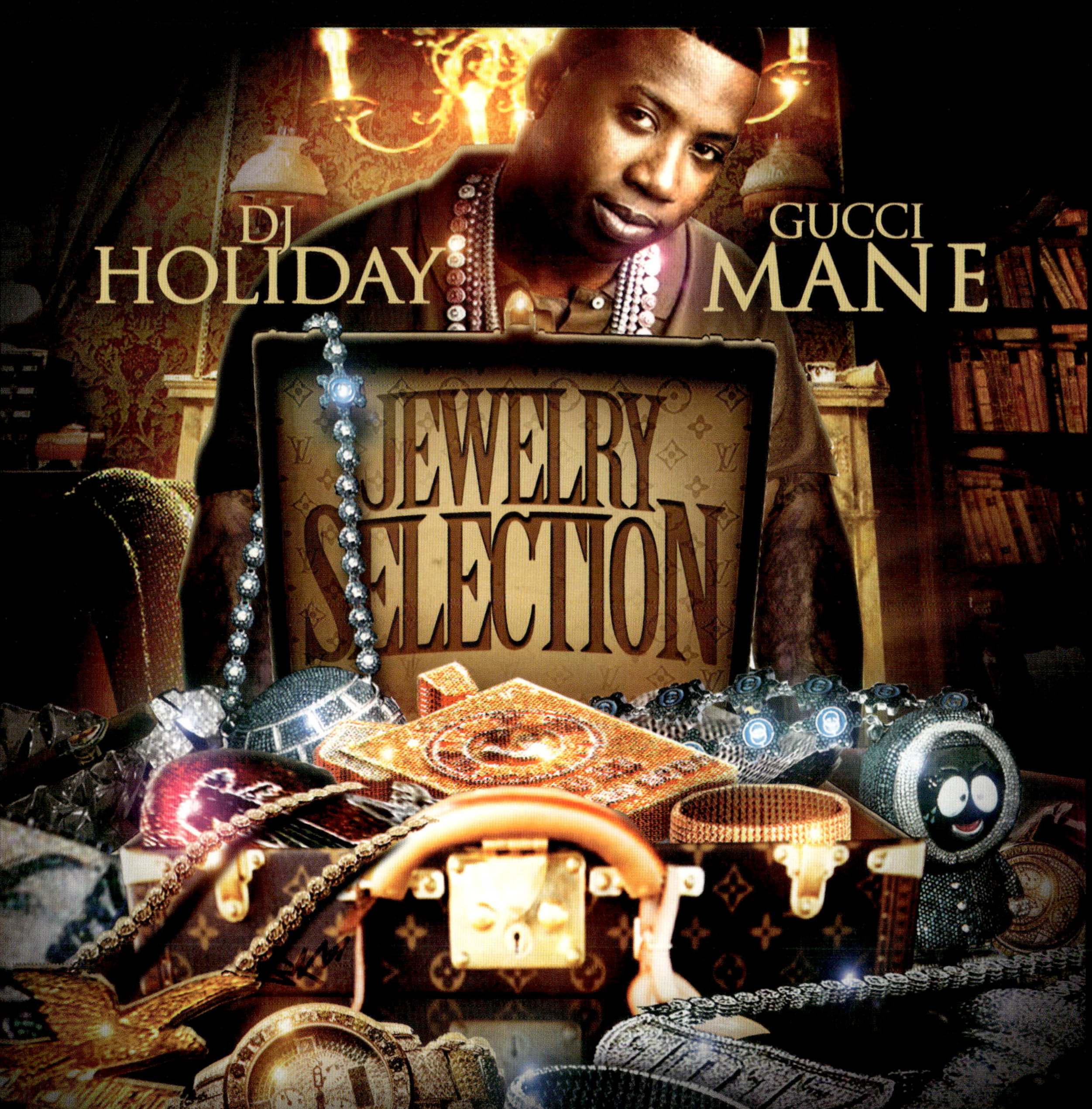

DJ Holiday & Gucci Mane
Jewelry Selection

Drake, Lil Wayne & Nicki Minaj
A Good Old Fashioned Orgy

Trey Songz
Trigga Lifestyle

Various Artists
Rnb Addiction Part Six

DJ Smallz
This That Southern Smoke! Vol. One

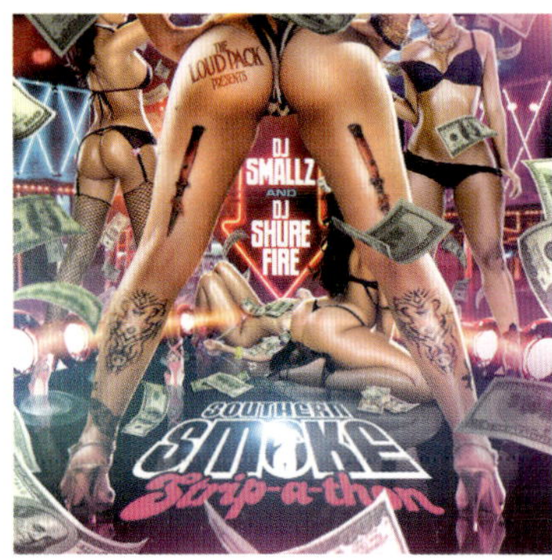

DJ Smallz & DJ Shure Fire
Southern Smoke Strip-A-Thon

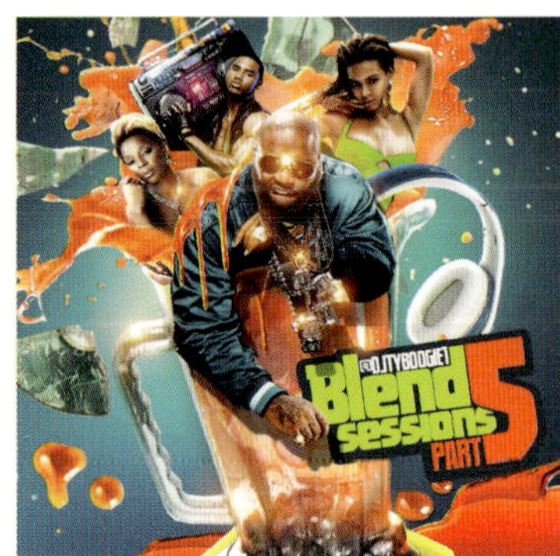

DJ Ty Boogie
Blend Sessions Part 5

Rick Ross
Here I Am!

DJ Storm
Drank Epidemic – I Don't Need No Host 23

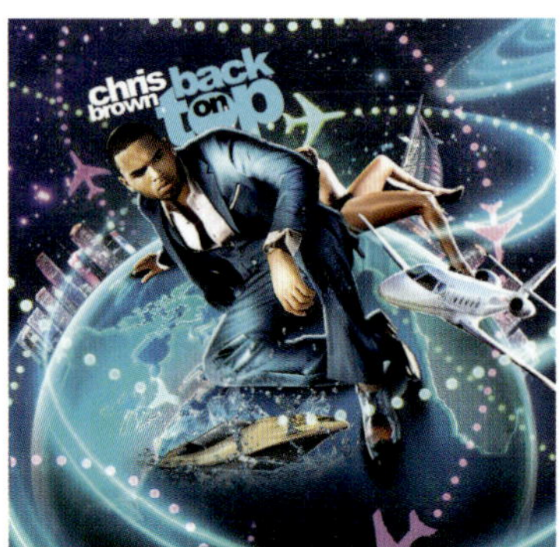

Chris Brown
Back on Top

T.I.
Kill Da Kang

Meek Mill & Rick Ross
The World Is Ours

DJ Smallz
Southern Smoke Civil War 4 - North vs South

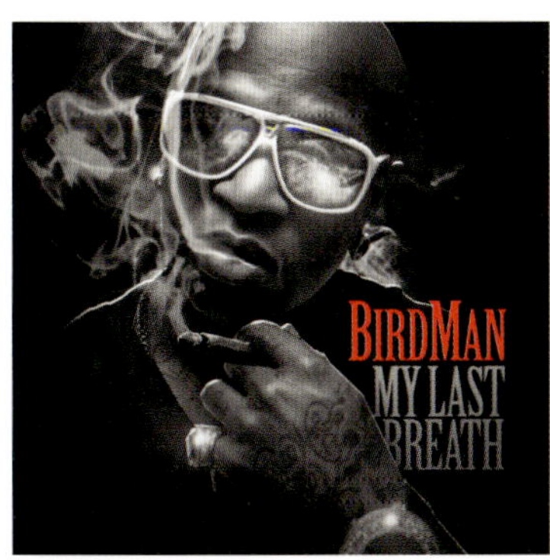

Birdman
My Last Breath

Gucci Mane presents
Bricksquad Mafia

Rick Ross, DJ Scream & Shaheem Reid
Rich Forever

Young Jeezy
Black Heart'd

Drake
I'm Not My Self

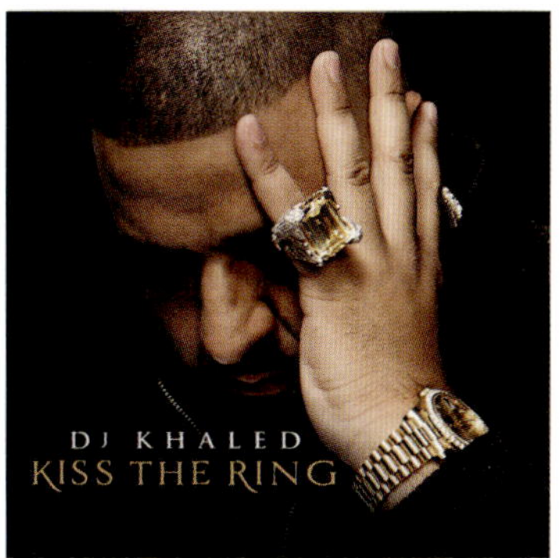

DJ Khaled
Kiss The Ring

Lil Wayne
The Devil Inside

Lil Wayne
Predator

Gucci Mane
Fuck The World

Various Artists
Block Muzik Pt. 5

Lil Wayne
Nothing To Lose

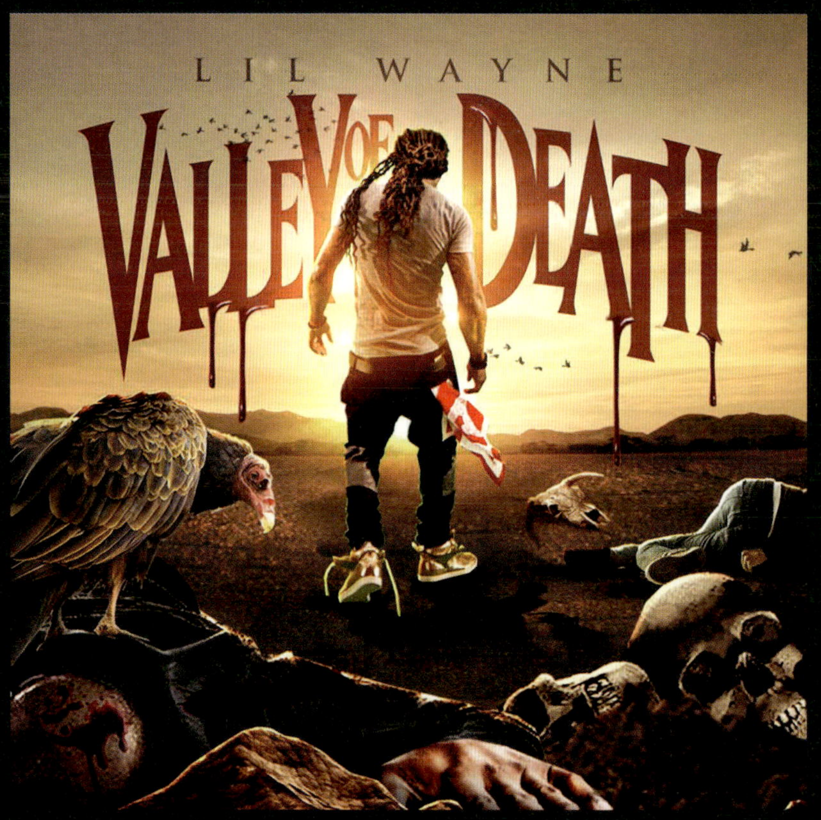

Lil Wayne
Valley Of Death

Team Run It presents Killa Kyleon
Lean On Me - The Adventures of Joe Clark

Maybach Music Group presents DJ Drama & Meek Mill
Dreamchasers

lighting effect? It's more about intuition. If I start to realize that it's not looking the way that I imagined, that's when I switch it up and when doing that the color scheme is definitely important. Even with designs that may not be realistic content-wise, like a guy standing on top of the moon, I want it to look as real as possible. So even in these hyperrealistic images, I try to maintain that level of realism. As if these situations would be possible.

You seem to put a lot of work into your typography.

I always want it to stand out and be realistic. I'm definitely a fan of designers that focus on typography, who can design their own font. I appreciate that. I'm not as adept as them but there has been instances where I've had a hard time finding fonts and I've had to illustrate the way I wanted it to look like. It's almost like creating a logotype for the title. It's also because of a lack of interesting fonts and some of those font collections are very expensive, too. If you want a specific font, you're looking to spend anywhere from 40-150 dollars. And it might not be worth it because it might be the only design that you'll use that particular font for.

Are there any other designers who you find inspiring?

If I had to pick somebody, I'd say Tansta. He was the one who actually pushed me to continue to go hard with the graphic design. I was always a fan of his work. He inspired me to keep the brand going. He was saying that there's a lot of projects to be done, there's a lot of new artists that's coming out there, and told me to keep doing it. He saw that I was talented enough to do something about it. And Tansta was a person whose designs I looked at and said *Wow, this dude is amazing!* He's really talented. And Miami Kaos, when it comes to graphic design, he is the originator. KidEight is talented too, he's definitely going hard. Me and him came up at the same time I think.

So you have good relationships with other designers?

If I have to be truthful, there's no real communication among other designers. If there is any type of communication, the ones I usually hear from are people trying to come up and they ask for my opinion. If they can study under me or if I can give them advice. That's pretty much it. The established ones, with them there's really no communication. I don't understand what the deal is with that, but that's the way it is.

Do you look at the situation as healthy competition?

That's what it is. But sometimes it would be nice if you could reach out to other people to get their opinions. I've had a few times that a designer hit me up asking for advice, but mostly it's very sour. We're competing against each other. Personally, I've never looked at it that way. I've looked at this as a hobby, that's how I've always felt about it. But there are times where I have been competitive, if I knew that an artist is doing a *Part 2* to a mixtape that I worked on and they're having another designer do it. Then a part of me says *I'm going to make sure this covers is ten times better than the others.* Overall, I don't look at it as straight up business. This is something that I'm doing on the side just to keep going. Something exciting.

If you lived one day inside a mixtape cover, what would that day look like?

There's a Lil Wayne cover of mine where I made it look like he was swimming. The idea was to make it look like a bridge had exploded and there was a riot going on in the background. But if you see the design, you see him coming out of the water. I thought something like that would look amazing for a music video. I've looked at some of my designs that way, that it would be a great music video. The explosions in the background, a nice car, nice females. A lot of music videos you see really try to aim for that movie look, and that's what I kept in mind for that cover.

I did a cover for The Empire for his series called *Southern Slang*. I made it look like they were breaking into a bank. The way I designed it was so efficient. That would be so dope, to see that and experience that in real. There's been a few covers I did that were more luxurious, in a mansion with money in front of the artists. I'd like to experience that too.

Could you please break down your favourite cover?

One of my favourite covers was *Dreamchasers 2*. That was a unique situation where I was dealing with the record label and the client had a specific direction in mind. I had done the first *Dreamchasers* cover for Meek Mill and that cover was definitely unique. It's really up there as one of my favourites. But what made this situation different is that when I did the first one, I came up with the idea of having him blow smoke out in the air. Since the title was *Dreamchasers*, I wanted him and DJ Drama in the smoke together with all of the different things that Meek is chasing, like cars, money and women. If you look closely at the design, it's very detailed. I've gotten a lot of business from that cover.

The client loved the first cover so much that they said *for the second one, we want it to be ten times better.* So the expectations were set higher and I had to challenge myself to pull it off. I would catch myself getting designer's block. I really didn't know how I could top that first design. I was going back and forth with the company. I would send a sketch but they didn't feel it. It got to the point where the client said *what you did with Dreamchasers, follow the same theme of smoke, abstract color, something vibrant but at the same time profound, like an album cover.* But I really couldn't follow their parameters, I had to do what I always do and that is what feels right.

Meek Mill
Dreamchasers 2

So I ended up using different pictures than the ones that they sent me to use. I decided that instead of seeing the artists surrounded by smoke and exhaling the smoke, it could be coming off them. The smoke should be coming out of their body from the side of their head. Initially, I tried doing something like a CAT scan, so you could see the brain and the jaw bone and you'd see what was going on in his head. If you look closely, you can see him and a group of other people on bikes. That's the life that he lives. He's really into that motocross lifestyle so I decided to put that into the design. I filled his head with stuff from the culture that he lives in.

At first, the design wasn't this close up. It was cut off at his torso and you could see his hand, and in his hand he was holding money. The money was kind of fading away with smoke coming out of it. But you really couldn't see what was going on in his head because it was too small. So I decided the money thing may not be that important, I could add it to the design elsewhere. If you look closely in the background, on the top of his head, you can see the hundred dollar bills. I incorporated it in the design after I made it bigger. They wanted something that was artsy and stood out and I really think that I pulled that off.

Tansta

Lil Wayne
Carter Crack Volume One

Raised during the hiphop boom of the 1990s, Brooklyn native Tansta has been immersed in its culture his whole life, a factor that's heavily influenced his creative work. His name, which he adopted during his graffiti days, was inspired by the rap world that he grew up in and would later go on to influence with his art. *I would write 'TAN' when I started doing graffiti. But when the rapper Fabolous came out in a song and said, "I'm a fabulous gangster" I started writing 'Fabulous Tansta' and sometimes just 'Tansta.' It stuck and later became my alias as a designer.*

Even though his upbringing and career is rooted in hiphop, Tansta refuses to let it define his artistic work and makes it clear that he's always trying to evolve and push his style in new directions. *All that was just part of the art for me. I drew, then I wrote graffiti, and then I started working with graphic design. I feel like it all begins with being an artist, trying to be creative and express yourself.* Though he believes that he's always had an artistic vision, Tansta can remember a specific moment, back in his seventh grade computer class, that put him on the path that led him to where he is today. *I opened up Photoshop and started creating random images. The teacher came over and asked if I had ever used the program, and I said no. So he asked 'how are you doing all this?' and I replied 'I don't know. I'm just testing things out, seeing how it goes, making things happen'. Every time I came to class after that, I was always doing my own work. The teacher saw what I was capable of so he let me go my own way and through that, it turned into a hobby. It only became a job after clients hit me up and gave me projects.* Tansta developed his skills in Photoshop Elements, the non-professional version of Adobe Photoshop. He was creating all his experiments using only the basic tools of the software, the way he still does to this day. *Photoshop now is insane. It cuts out a face for you automatically, removing all the background. I still don't know how to use it all. I'm getting a hang of it even if I'm doing everything manually.*

Tansta admits that he wasn't some sort of a Photoshop prodigy and that his style is the result of countless hours of hard work. *When I began, I wasn't good. I understood how things should look, perspective and things like that. But you have to practice and practice until you get better. It wasn't until later on when I realised I could actually create something. That I could take someone's picture, put it on a background, and make it look like that was the real picture.*

Tansta found inspiration in the mixtape covers that he saw in the streets but he also had a strong love for movie posters. He remembers his first encounter with a cover that looked like a movie poster designed by Nojo, a mixtape cover pioneer. *It was clean, it was crisp. That inspired me to try to make artwork that looked like movie posters.* As Tansta honed his style, he began getting recognition on online forums. *I started posting work in the graphics section of the forum work and gradually I got better and with that the response from other forum members improved too. Eventually, some people not on the forums began to notice me and I started getting offered some projects. And the projects just kept coming in. I always say that if you put the work in, it will speak for itself. That's what I did.* Tansta's designs became so demanded that eventually he had to start turning down projects. *I did hundreds of covers. I did so many that I reached a point where I couldn't really do any more. In the past two or three years, I've done maybe less than a hundred covers a year, as opposed to 2005 to 2008 where I made over a thousand.*

While Tansta has become one of the leading mixtape designers in the industry, he holds a unique perspective about the industry and his role within it. He seems pessimistic about many aspects of the culture and openly shares his opinions on what's wrong with the visual world that he's become such an instrumental part of. *Sometimes these rappers want something creative but there's only so much I can really do. These guys aren't even remotely creative in their lyrics, but they want me to be creative for them. There are times when the cover is a lot better than the music on the mixtape. It's ridiculous. Plenty of times I went and got the mixtape I designed the cover for, listened to it and felt 'Wow, this is really garbage'. It's basically what led me to cut down on doing covers because I want to be doing them for a good reason. I know that at the end of the day it's a job, but if it's wearing on me and I'm draining my energy for garbage, I'm not gonna do it. I feel that as an artist, I need some kind of self-respect.*

When reflecting upon his career, it's clear that Tansta feels like he's outgrown the mixtape industry and aims to move forward as an artist. *I always say that you have to be versatile. You can't just be one-dimensional, which is something that the mixtape industry can make you.* This feeling has lead Tansta into new creative ventures to establish himself as a more multifaceted artist that isn't stuck in the rap game that he's become disillusioned with over the years. During our conversation, he expresses much of his criticisms of the mixtape industry and how he feels that it has somewhat limited his creativity. However, despite his frustrations, Tansta isn't bitter about his time in the mixtape game and admits how grateful he is to have found success in this niche world of graphic design. *In a sense, mixtapes might have saved me because before I started doing this I was getting into a lot of trouble. I was getting into a lot of fights and I did dumb shit. But then I started working and occupying my time with this. So while a lot of my old friends that I stopped hanging out with, some of which are dead now, were turning into junkies or criminals, graphic design kept me away from that. It helped me to escape the negativity.*

You do a lot less work now. Can you describe the creative process and how it has changed over the years?

I've stopped doing so many covers because I started losing creativity. There's only so much you can do and there's only so much subject matter that you can work with in the rap game. And personally, as a hiphop fan, I like a lot of the artists that most people don't even listen to anymore, like Nas or Big L. Now people are into Rick Ross, which is cool but that's not the music that I prefer to listen to. Still, I'm making Rick Ross covers to left and right. It didn't really motivate me like the times I'd get a project for an artist that I like. For a Nas or Talib Kweli cover, I put in overtime and I try to be really creative. For others, like Rick Ross, there's not so much creativity. What do you do? Add drugs, money, some half-naked girls with big butts. That's really all there is, that's all they want.

You feel cornered with drugs and big butts. What kind of creative process do you prefer, freedom or limitations?

I do like freedom but some ideas help. It doesn't have to be *I need the cover to be like this and like that and like this.* Maybe just a general idea or concept. Out of that, I can find something that usually helps me moving. As opposed to briefs like *I need the hottest cover ever. Here's the info and here's the money. And I need it in 24 hours.* I've started charging extra for that. I was hustled to a point where I couldn't do that anymore. Especially me being young, I was doing all this when I was 17. I'm 23 now but I started doing this at a young age and eventually I couldn't do it anymore. I couldn't keep up and on top of that you have a lot of new

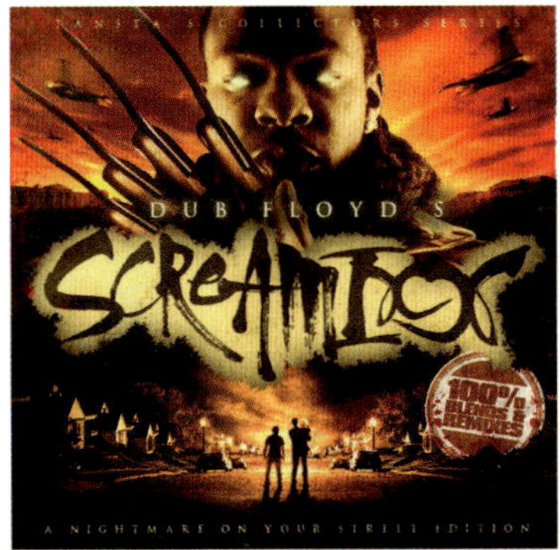

Dub Floyd
Screamixx

Big Mike presents Raw Doggz
Take Over The World

Big Mike presents Raw Doggz
The Future

Big Mike presents Raw Doggz
Revolution

Chaundon & Mr Peter Parker
Venom

DJ Spinz & Pretty Boy Tank
Space Invaders 2

Tapemasters Inc.
This Is Hiphop 5

DJ Hitz
I'm So NY Part 2

DJ G-Spot
Justo Would be Proud

Plies & Rick Ross
Goon Music 2

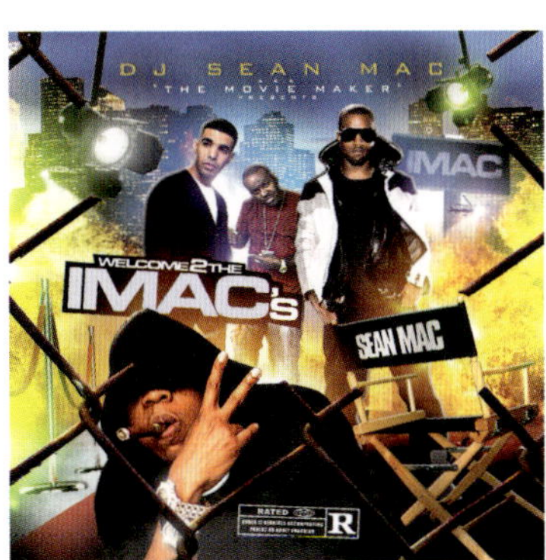

DJ Sean Mac
Welcome 2 the Imac's

Benzi presents Joe Budden
We Got The Remix - Mood Muzik 3

The Apphilliates & Bad Boy South/Block Ent. present Gorilla Zoe & DJ Holiday
Feeding Time

DJ Hitz
Laugh Now Cry Later 3

Various Artists
We The Best

DJ Hitz & Lil Wayne
It's The Remix Baby

DJ Sean Mac presents Bump J
Dinner Time! "Let's Eat"

Consequence
Movies On Demand

The Hitmen, Tapemasters Inc. & Fabolous
Loso's World

Big Mike, DJ Thoro & Lil Wayne
The Carter After The Carter

DJ Kronik, Papa Smirf & Flo Rida
Freestyle Kronikles

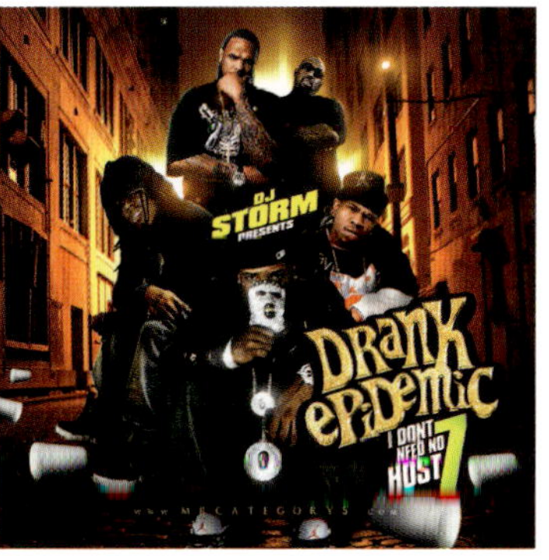

DJ Storm presents
Drank Epidemic – I Don't Need No Host 7

Lil Wayne
Americas Most Wanted 2

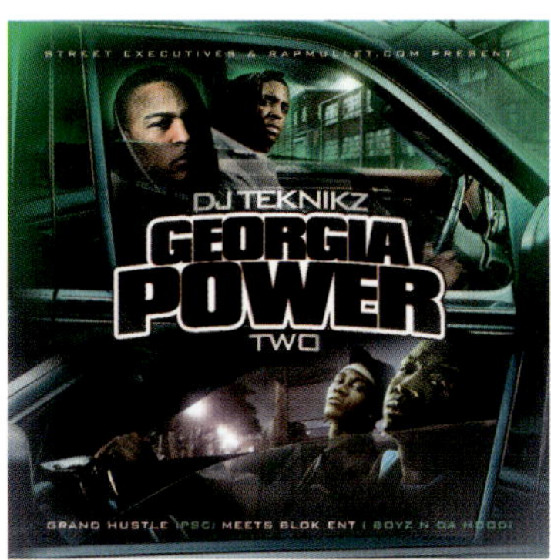

Street Executives & Rapmullet.com present DJ Teknikz
Georgia Power Two

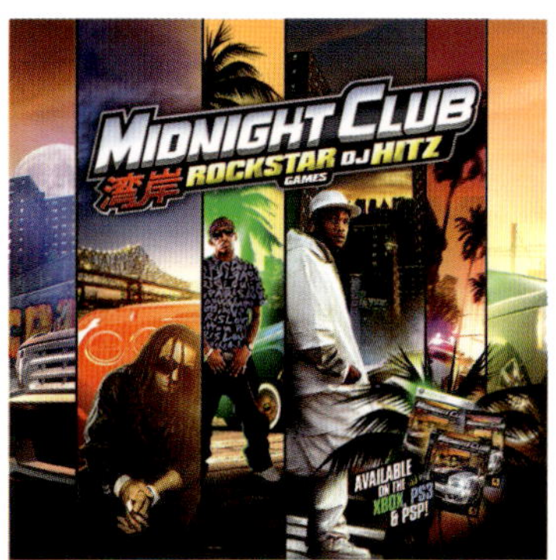

DJ Hitz
Midnight Club

Cocaine City presents French Montana
Live From Africa

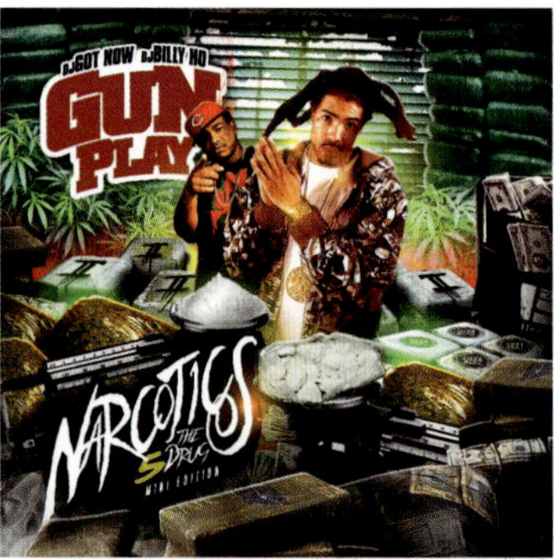

DJ Got Now, DJ Billy Ho & Gunplay
Narcotics the Drug 5

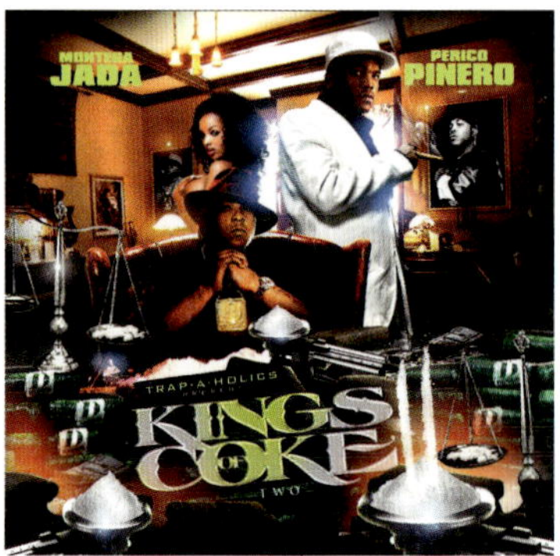

Trap-A-Holics present Montega Jada & Perico Pinero
Kings Of Coke Two

designers coming up and they make work that looks like yours, but it's not. But to the average DJ, it wouldn't even matter. It looks like it, so it will pass. Typically the big name DJs only want the quality, but the DJs that are out there for the quick buck usually just want something that looks close to it. It doesn't have to be all perfect, the text doesn't have to be lined up as good as it could be. Small things that I personally think means a lot.

How do you react to people imitating your style?

Well, no idea is original. Everybody is inspired by each other. At the same time, it's also a form of respect. There's one thing if you jock someone. But if you just take small elements from a certain artist but blend it into your own style, that's art in its purest form. Everybody takes a little bit of something they've seen along the way and tries to make it their own.

How's your relationship to other designers?

I have nothing but the outmost respect for those designers that put in all the work the way I did. Say Miami Kaos, he put in more work than I ever did. On top of that, he's a lot older, he's much more established, he's well known. Compared to him, I'm nowhere. He's the type of designer that I really respect. His dedication and consistency. I actually met Miami Kaos in person. When I was still making a lot of covers, he was only beginning. Then I stepped away and saw him making covers everywhere. I'm not saying it's just because I moved away but I have to think that it probably helped a little bit.

Do you feel like the direction the mixtape game has been moving is negative, regarding creativity?

Just look at the music. I feel that five years ago, it was a bit better than it is now. Now it's all about money, all about getting paid. It's not like it wasn't about that back then but there was a sense of passion and creativity. Trying to make something nice where people go *Wow!* But now it's just like, *Ehh, just a cover.*

What do you think is needed for that creativity to return?

DJs. Because they're the ones who get the covers made. Better, creative tapes. Because now all the mixtapes are about Rick Ross and Lil Wayne. The DJs that I like are DJ Dirty Harry, DJ Neil Armstrong, DJ Green Lantern. Green Lantern used to have these ugly ass covers. But one time, I was already doing a lot of work, but I was bored so I sent him a message saying *Hit me up. I'll do a cover. It will be an*

Young Jeezy
That Hard White

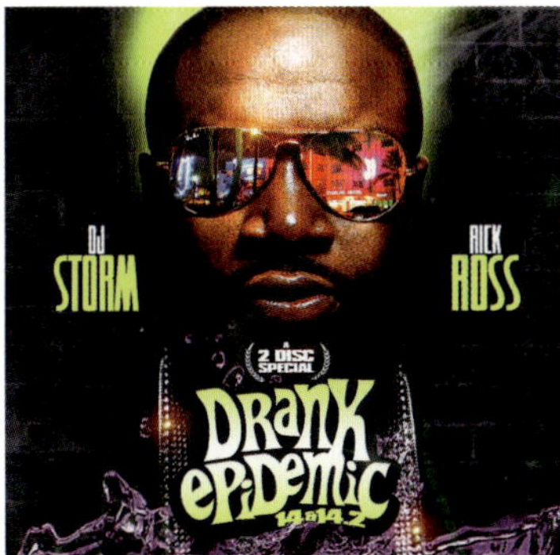

DJ Storm & Rick Ross
Drank Epidemic 14 & 14.2

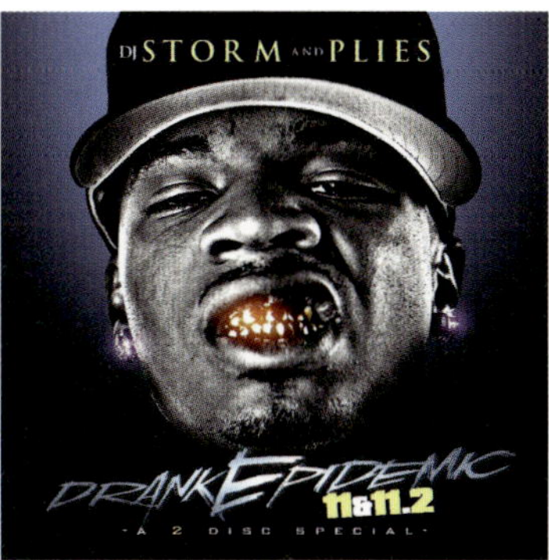

DJ Storm & Plies
Drank Epidemic 11 & 11.2

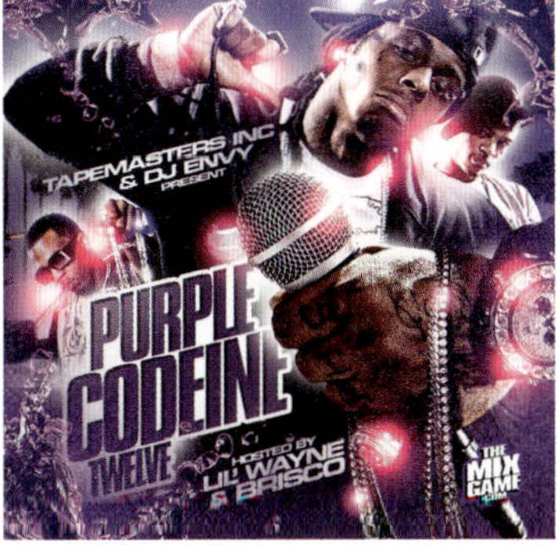

Tapemasters Inc. & DJ Envy
Purple Codeine Twelve

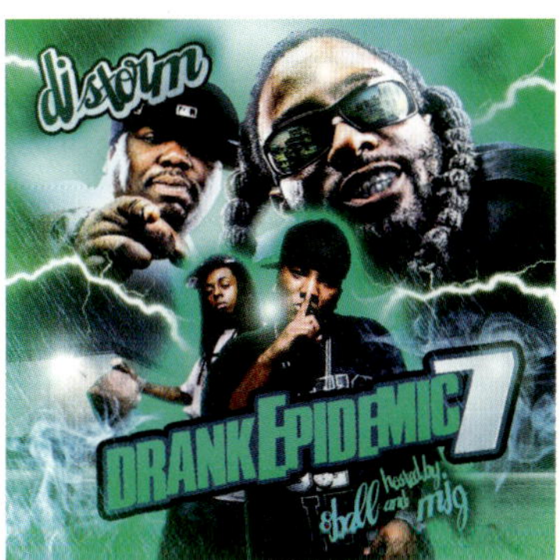

DJ Storm
Drank Epidemic 7

DJ Roz presents
Olde English "800" – Drinkin Music

honour. I have a lot of Green Lantern tapes and I listen to them a lot, so it's a respect thing. And after seeing some of his covers, I thought that I could make something better in 15 minutes. That's the only time I actually went out and asked someone for an opportunity to do work for them just out of respect. But every DJ now is just like every other DJ.

While we don't see any graffiti in your covers, would you say that it's a part of your work?

Yes. It's there in the way I work with colours. The way I'm using brushes. It's almost like drawing, like painting.

Your style is clean, almost glossy.

Again, I basically look at movie posters and album covers. There you see the quality of how it's crisp and everything fits right. It doesn't look forced. Every time I get a picture, I always touch it up. It's never the same picture in the end, I never just put it on the cover. I do a lot to it before it's ready.

Can you describe the technical side of your work?

I just start as I've always done, just trial and error. I try something and if I like it, I just keep going. And if I don't, I try something else. I would open the same file six times and try six different things and see which ones I like. I just keep going with it and eventually I have a final cover. I use the pencil tool mainly. It's an annoying process. There are some pictures where it's easy for me, but there are some that are very hard. Say you have to cut out the whole car and all the little details that comes with it. Or, let's say, a chain where you have to remove all the holes in each piece of the link. It can get very tedious. It's a tedious kind of job.

With all of the covers that you've produced, it's impressive that you try so many different alternatives and then pick the best one.

Well, I'm not saying that I make six versions of everything. If it's a legit album cover for an actual release, that's one thing. For a mixtape, that's almost asking too much. If anything, I would open up two files and use different kinds of images of the same artist and see what I can come up with. Sometimes I can sit there for hours and not come up with anything, that's the artist's block. A lot of times, I try to either open up something new and try something else, or just pause and free my mind up a little bit.

Evil Empire presents
Interstate Trafficking Volume Six

Evil Empire & DJ Woogie
The Unit Remains Supreme

DJ Kronik
Southern Clientele

DJ Billy Ho, DJ Got Now & Pitbull
The Streets Are Talking

Evil Empire & Cam'ron
Criminal Minded

DJ Holiday & Lil Scrappy
The Grustle

Hell Rell & 40 Cal
Year Of The Gun

The Empire presents DJ 5150
Goon Music

Follow The Future presents The Game & DJ Roz
Comptons Most Wanted 2

Jadakiss, Tapemasters Inc. & Cam'ron
The City Ain't The Same

DJ Got Now, DJ Kriz Stylez, DJ Billy Ho & The Game
Can't Leave Rap Alone The West Needs Me 2

Brisco, DJ Kronik & DJ Obscene
Black Bags & Yellow Tape

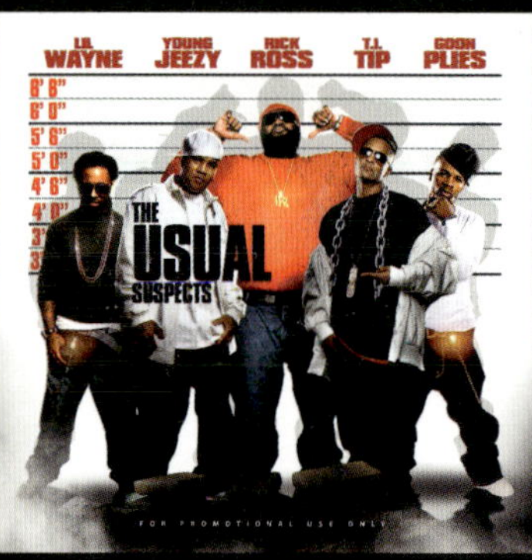

Lil Wayne, Young Jeezy, Rick Ross, T.I. & Plies
The Usual Suspects

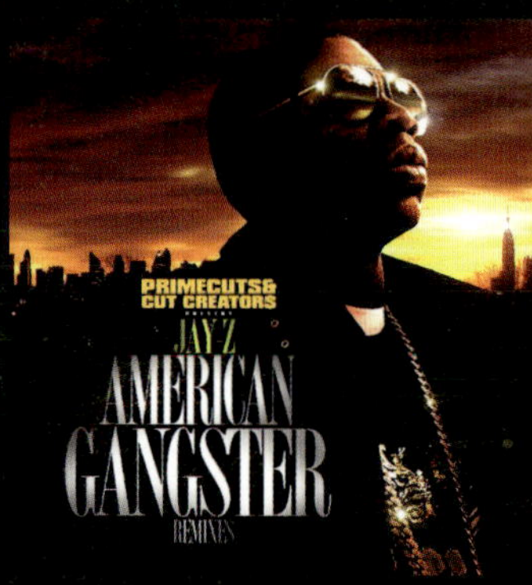

Primecuts & Cut Creators present Jay-Z
American Gangster Remixes

DJ Billy Ho presents Smitty

Lil Wayne and Friends

Evil empire, DJ Plus & DJ E Stacks

DJ
GOT NOW
DJ
BILLY HO
THREE
SIX
MAFIA
WE RUN
MEMPHIS
HOSTED BY
DJ PAUL

Evil Empire & Cocaine City presents
Cocaine Trafficking 2 – The Coke Wave Prequel

Tapemasters Inc. & DJ Envy present
Purple Codeine Part 14

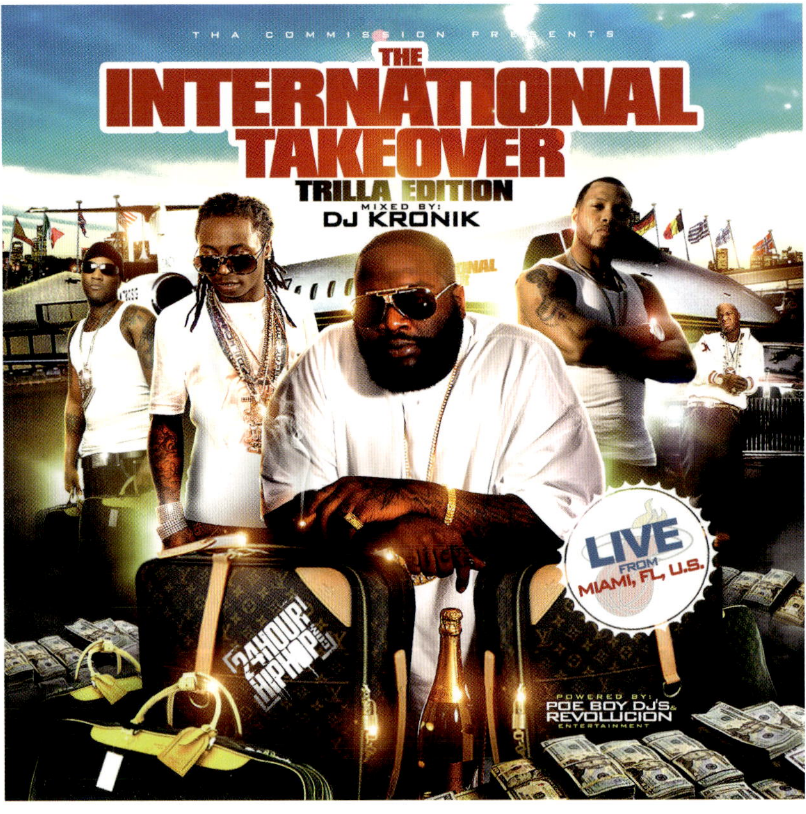

Tha Commission presents
The International Takeover – Trilla Edition

The Usual Suspects present Rick Ross
It's a Movie Baby

Flo Rida
Goin Postal – Freestyle Kronikles 3

DJ Scream & MLK present
Hoodrich Radio – Most Requested Five

DJ Drama & Soulja Boy
Gangsta Grillz – Follow Me

DJ E Stacks & Mistah F.A.B
Mr Youtube AKA Google Me

Bizkit & Tapemasters Inc. present Lil Boosie & Gucci Mane
Who's Got The Crown Volume Four

Is it important for you that there is a connection between the music and the cover? Do you always hear the music beforehand?

A lot of times, they give me their thing so I can listen to it and hear the lyrics. Just to get an understanding of what they're talking about, what they're about. So when I make the cover, I have all these elements in my head and I can just put a cover together with all these details, like a certain building or certain car, things that describe the artist. I mean, if anything, that just makes my job easier, to work with direct references.

For a while there were so many distinct visual references in mixtape cover. Such as during the 2008 presidential election there were tons of Obama covers. But we don't see that much today. Why is that?

I remember when Obama was running, in the beginning, it was a big deal. But for the second term, personally, I knew he was going to win. I felt like anyone with any common sense knew he was going to win. But when he was first coming there was plenty of covers. The *Vote or Die* series and many more covers in that same style.

It was around that time, 2008 and before, when something would happen in the news and the next week there would be a mixtape cover based on it.

Yeah, that was when Mick Boogie was doing a lot of tapes. That was when a lot of DJs that don't even bother with mixtapes anymore were actually making consistent and good mixtapes. If you've ever heard *God's Gift* with Mick Boogie and Joey Fingaz, I made that cover and it's one of my favourite tapes ever. That tape is beautiful. The way they made it is amazing. Mick Boogie always wanted creative covers. He never wanted a cover that looked someone else's. There were plenty of times where I gave him covers that looked like someone else's and he just said *come on, you know I can't have that.* And I said *my bad.* I feel like you probably don't have DJs like that around anymore. People who would actually be like *I have to be honest with you, that's not what I need.*

What visual trends have inspired you over the years?

There was a trend in 2007 and 2008 that was all about color. Everything had to have mad colors. *If the cover doesn't have a lot of colors, then I don't want it.* That's how it was. If you look at a lot of my covers, they're very colorful. Not all of them, but a lot of them have a lot of color so they stand out. Eventually it got a little silly. Like what are they, clown covers?

What do you think is dominating the mixtape world today? It seems like everything got a lot cleaner.

Now it's at a point where there are so many resources out there to take that anyone can make a nice, clean cover. You can download Photoshop files and effects. You can take all these other covers that are already made for inspiration. The formula is there now, so when there's a new designer coming up, everything is laid out for him. I feel like mixtape covers are easy now. It takes a lot less effort to make them today.

As you're limiting the amount of mixtape covers you create, what is the new direction for your work?

I'm trying to do more commercial stuff. Something more stabile, not as erratic as the mixtape business. They come and go. At the end of the day, it's freelance work. So being a freelance designer, you get projects, you do them, you get paid and then you move on. But even as a freelancer, the best thing to do is to establish a consistency with a client. He gives you a project, and if you do it well, he keeps coming back.

When you talk about moving on from the mixtape industry, is it because you feel somewhat artistically confined?

The thing about mixtape covers is that people want a lot, whereas, I think that it's better to be cleaner. To keep it simple and on point. I feel like if you have to much going on in your cover, it's stupid. It's a little image and you're going to have so much going on in it that takes the focus away. There are some covers where there's a lot going on but when you look at all the details, it's still cool. But that doesn't go for every cover and it kind of became a habit for DJs to ask for everything. *Let me get cars, let me get money, let me get drugs, let me get all this.* And you think *Wow, how is this all going to fit and seem realistic?*

Have there been elements that you have been requested to include that you just felt were too far out?

Yes, pounds of drugs just laying on the floor or money laying on the concrete. Where does that happen? I feel dumb because I used to put that shit in my covers. I look at it now and feel like *What the fuck! This is stupid. It doesn't make sense. Who would do this? Who would leave thousands of dollars in the street in the hood?*

I'll even tell DJs that I'll do a cover for them but I'm not going to have random money or drugs on the floor. If it's cold-ass weather in the image, I'm not going to have butt-naked bitches in there. If it's not going to make sense, I'm just not going to do it. So now when clients says they need money on the cover, I might have to add a table or something that can hold the money so at least it makes some kind of sense.

You're adding realism to mixtape covers.

That's how it should be because it got a little too crazy. It became a fairytale. Rap is very fairytale-like. All of these

Black Jab Music presents Panama
Panama vs The Industry – Ring Side Seats – The Weigh-In

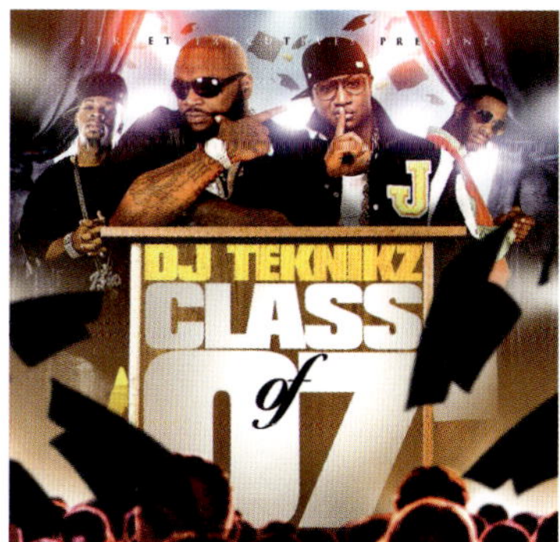

DJ Teknikz
Class of 07

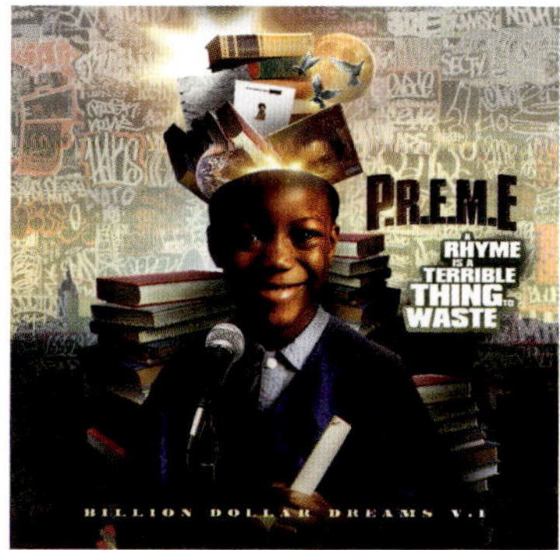

P.R.E.M.E – *A Rhyme Is A Terrible Thing To Waste*
Billion Dollar Dreams V.1

Statik Selektah, Royce 5'9 & DJ Premier
The Bar Exam

DJ Got Now, DJ Papa Smirf & T.I.
Bankhead Ambassador

DJ Hitz & Neyo
The Prince Of R&B One

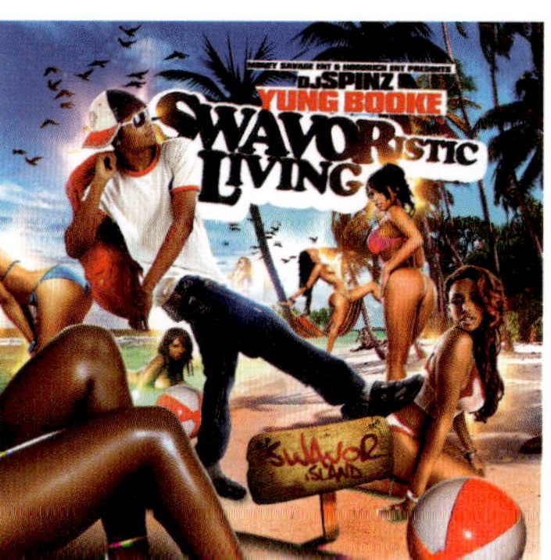

DJ Spinz & Yung Booke
Swavoristic Living

Tapemasters Inc. & The Untouchables
The Future Of R'N'B 22

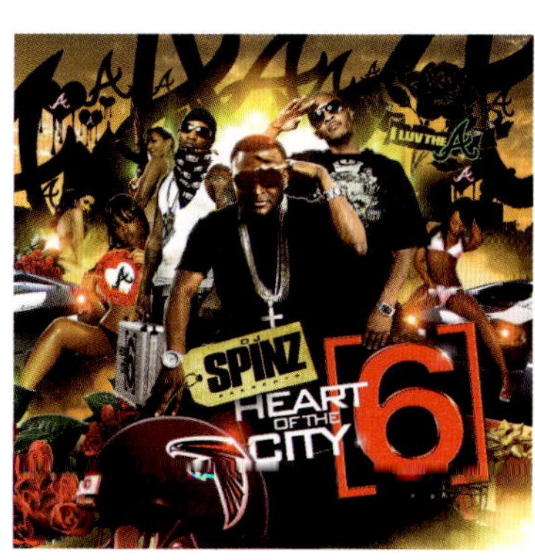

DJ Spinz presents
Heart Of The City 6

DJ Spinz presents
American Diva

The Usual Suspects present Ludacris
Blockbuster 6

Akon & Tapemasters Inc.
One Man Band Man

Benzi & The Knocks present
American G Funk

DJ Hitz presents Dipset Byrd Gang
Life In The Fastlane Part 1

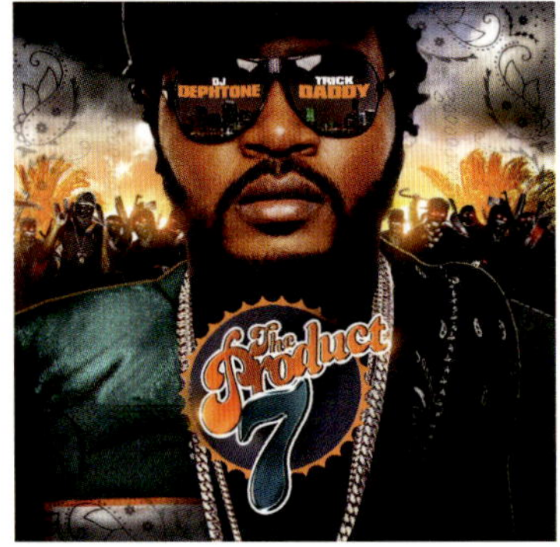

DJ Depthone & Trick Daddy
The Product 7

Street Executives & Hood Affairs present DJ Teknikz
Georgia Power – Grand Hustle vs CTE

Birdman, Lil Wayne & Mixtrap.com presents
Happy Fathers Day

Your Favorite Suppliers present Lil Wayne
The Leak 2

DJ Dub Floyd, DJ Smooth Denali & DJ Unexpected
Hiphop University Series – The 5th Element

rappers don't even live most of this shit that they rap about. These guys are basically reporters, reporting on what other criminals are doing, not themselves. It's what others are doing. It's silly.

If you would live one day inside the world of one of your mixtape covers what would that day look like?

Apparently, what that would look like is that I'd be filthy rich, I'd be a drug lord. I'd have extremely hot women at my disposal and I'd have massive amounts of luxury cars.

And all your cash would definitely be on the table?

Definitely, now it would be on the table. Five years ago, the money would be all over the ground with all my friends around. Just because I trust them with hundreds of thousands of dollars.

I know, I know. It's silly. That's why I can't do this shit anymore. At the same time, I haven't exactly been in a position where I needed all this work. I chose to work. I'm not saying I'm rich, I'm not. I'm saying this because I was designing when I was 16 years old. You got people that are 25 who are designing to pay their rent. I was designing to buy myself some new shoes.

Do you feel that moving away from mixtapes is a process of maturing as an artist?

I'm not like Miami Kaos. I don't animate my covers. He's going to stay in the game because he's such a big part of it. Something I cannot say I am. So he can keep doing his thing. He's been doing this before I came in the game, before anyone who's doing covers came in the game.

But you can't do mixtape covers forever. It's not a job that you want to do forever, I think. Because at the end of the day, it's freelance. You're not on a contract, you're not guaranteed anything. There was a time, in the beginning, when I didn't even take down payments. Eventually, I wouldn't start doing a cover if I didn't have some kind of insurance that I would get paid. There was plenty of times where I finished a project and sent it to a clients then never heard from them again. For all I know, they could have taken that small preview, blown it up and had someone else to do the back cover.

Since you didn't need to do this to pay the rent when you first started, what was your driving force?

I had a girlfriend, that was my drive. It was also the fact that I didn't grow up with a lot of things. While my friends had Playstations and Nintendo 64's, I had a Sega Genesis. There came a point when I was 14 or 15 where I was tired of that

The Empire & Lil Wayne
The Drought Is Over 5

DJ Kris Styles, DJ L-Gee, DJ Big Mike & Young Life
Hard Knock Life – The Black & White Print Edition

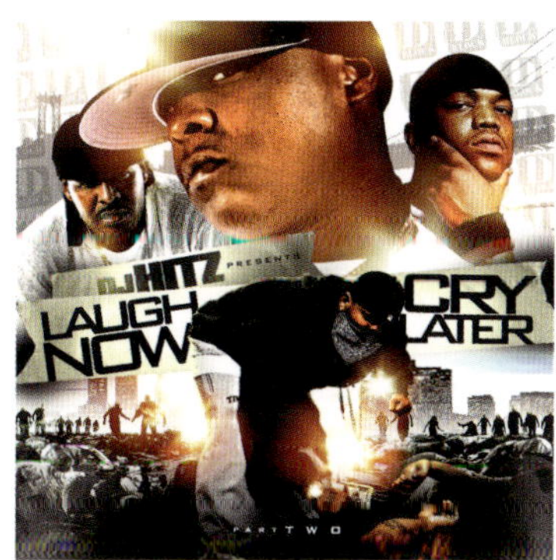

DJ Hitz presents
Laugh Now Cry Later Part Two

shit. So I started working, and from the money I made I bought a new TV, a new car, anything I needed.

You said how you refuse things that are stupid in your work and also how you moved away from negativity in your personal life. Do you feel there's a connection between those aspects of yourself?

Yeah, that's kind of how it was. I did the covers, I got response, I got feedback. It wasn't just clients. I'd post them up on forums and I'd get tons of views and tons of comments and everybody said that it was dope. I got nothing but love. And I show love, if people needed help, I tried to help. But at the same time, I'm not a teacher. No one taught me, I taught myself. That's kind of how it was, I did work, people showed me love, and that helped me. If people would have said that it was garbage, I probably wouldn't have kept doing it.

A lot of DJs and rap artists would tell you the same thing. Everyone that comes from a certain area. People are just hard headed. Criminal activity, criminal mischief, all that. Robbery and gang activity. Just shit that would probably mess your life up. So people probably try to acknowledge that they have talent and try to use it and better themselves. Better their mental state. That definitely helped me, just like it helps the basketball player who grows up in the hood and instead of going with his homeboys that only care about smoking weed and having sex with certain girls and acting cool, he says *Man screw that I'ma go hit the gym.* So that's what I was doing, but through design. I was doing that and I was making money. I sometimes imagine if I wasn't doing this and not making money. What would I be doing? Robbing? I had friends who robbed some people and asked me to join them. But instead I would put some work in and the week after I had a new pair of shoes.

Can you choose one of your favourite covers and guide us through the concept and how you executed it?

If I get the right photos, I can usually make something good. A lot of the times when I have a bad photo, that's when I have to get creative and improvise. Take that photo and make a new photo, manipulate it, adding a new body, things like that. But there's a cover that I made from absolutely nothing. It was *The Drought Is Over 5*. It basically looks like it's Lil Wayne in front of a night club. I wouldn't say it's one of my favourite covers, but just the fact that I made this out of a bunch of images. I made that whole thing out of random things, the framed plaques with the covers, things inside the building and all that. I basically just freestyled it and came up with this. I thought of a club type of scenery. It sucks though, I'm looking at it now and feel that I could've done so much better, so much I could fix. But we're talking about something I made six years ago, so obviously I could do a much better job today.

The Black Wall Street presents XO
Slugz-N-Stitchez

Trap-A-Holics present Lil Boosie & Lil Wayne
Battle For The Bayou

Skrilla

Shoot 5 Ent. presents Plies
Return Of The Real

In an industry flooded with self-taught Adobe Photoshop users pumping out covers, Skrilla is of the rare breed of formally trained graphic designers. After enrolling in a two-year design program, he developed his Photoshop skills in college, where his work tended to gravitate towards his love of hiphop. *I was always looking through magazines like The Source to find cool images. I think I convinced my teacher to let me do a poster for some kind of live show event as an assignment. I remember scanning images from The Source of Bad Boy Entertainment artists like P. Diddy and I put them together with text and background using the computer. It looked awful and basic but when I look back at it today, it's obvious that it was me experimenting and exploring using what skills I had at the time.*

While many other mixtape designers have their roots in graffiti, Skrilla grew up reading comic books and trying to emulate the images he saw in them. *When I was younger, I was always drawing. Even through my teenage years, I loved reading and drawing comics. I don't really do that anymore but that was definitely a huge part of my early love for design and art.* Despite his education, Skrilla attributes his success as a designer, to his focus and hard work outside of the classroom. *We learned the basics of graphic design in college.*

But I think it's something you pick up over time. A lot of it is about experimenting and just looking at design.

Another interesting aspect of Skrilla's work is his physical and personal distance from the rap world that he's become a part of, being a Brit based in Birmingham, England. Unlike fellow UK designer KidEight, Skrilla has visited the States but not related to his work, so he remains very detached from the environments that his clients come from. *The design industry is a perfect example of how the internet has changed the world, because what I'm doing now would not have been possible 15 years ago. Through the internet, you can get in contact with anyone in the world. National borders and countries, they've just become irrelevant with internet. Being halfway around the world isn't a problem. Even getting paid. With PayPal, it's just so easy and convenient. There is no money changing hands so it makes it possible to work with anyone no matter where they're located.* Skrilla doesn't see his distance from the predominantly American rap industry as something negative, but instead finds it inspiring to be a part of it from another corner of the planet. *It's an amazing feeling to be doing projects and work with people globally.*

Despite Skrilla's geographic separation from his clients, his relentless work ethic, along with the perfect timing of his mixtape pursuits, made his entrance into the industry quite seamless. *I would find the names and e-mail addresses of DJs and promoters online and on the back of CDs and magazines and stuff. I sent out emails asking if they needed work and I succeeded, people got back to me. Back then, there was a lot less junk mail, so people would respond to emails a lot quicker than they do now. Nowadays, people's inboxes get full from so many offers. So it kind of stood out when I started emailing DJs about artwork.* Skrilla got his first paid project while still at university with a comic book inspired design, that caught the eye of DJ P-Cutta. *It was a 'Grand Theft Auto'-style cover because back then that style of characters were quite popular. I had done a few of designs based on 'Grand Theft Auto' artwork and sent them out to some DJs whose contacts info I had collected. DJ P-Cutta hit me back and asked me if he could use my artwork for his 'Street Wars Vol. 12' mixtape and it just went on from there. I hadn't even really thought about doing this as a profession and suddenly I got this paid project for a rather big DJ, so I thought 'Wow, I can go somewhere with this'.*

Since his cross-Atlantic breakthrough into the mixtape industry, Skrilla has earned his place as one of the most prolific designers, producing work for some of the biggest names in hiphop and remaining so busy that he has no idea how many mixtape covers he's designed. *I've been doing it since 2006 or 2007, so it's got to be hundreds now. I've got covers that I can't even remember designing.* Although it might seem strange for a young British kid to dedicate years of his life to creating images of extravagant rap fantasies and gangster lifestyles, Skrilla keeps a balanced perspective on his work. *Even though we're making all these things that are very street and hood, a lot of us designers have never been to the hood. But you get influenced by the music and the visuals that the music paints. To a certain extent, you can get caught in a bubble with it. But you can't get too caught up in it because no graphic designer out there is selling drugs, hustling, pimping or doing anything these rappers are doing. So you've got to have a knowledge about the subjects but stay very distant at the same time. What the rappers talk about in their lyrics, is of course a different world than my reality, but it's something you've got to absorb and use for your imagination. My family and friends are really amused by it. You know, you got pictures of girls with huge breasts and huge asses and money, drugs and everything. It's a completely different world. It's part of what makes the mixtape design game so unique.*

While Skrilla can find amusement in his position within the hiphop world, it's clear that he takes his work seriously and has a deep respect for the covers that he creates. Although other designers, such as Tansta, have expressed their occasional irritation with some of the imagery that they're commissioned to produce, Skrilla seems thoroughly satisfied to be working with the extreme side of mixtape cover aesthetic. *I think that what you put in a cover doesn't have to reflect reality at all. So if you limit yourself to thinking 'this wouldn't happen in real life', you would probably get quite boring covers. That's the great thing about it. You let your imagination go crazy and you're allowed to bring out your wildest ideas. If you look at mixtape design, it's an artform. It is art, and art is not conformist. It can be anything you want.*

Do you remember when you first started getting interested in doing music-related design?

From very early on, with albums, I always loved to listen to the music but also looking through the booklet. That's something that appealed to me, I loved the artwork. I remember buying a few albums just based on the artwork alone. So I was always interested in that kind of thing and when I saw mixtape covers, that was something special. The design was just completely different from regular album artwork. It was still called artwork but it was more hip and edgy and more urban. It was very street. And when I saw these very early mixtapes coming out on the internet, it was definitely around the time I first got on the internet, I thought *Wow, this is really cool, really detailed.* And you know they're not official, so they can use images from wherever they want. There was a lot of manipulated movie posters that were turned into mixtape covers, with rappers faces on things. So I thought that since I knew how to use Photoshop, I should have a little play around with this.

Around what time is this?

Probably the early 00s. I remember when the mixtape industry boomed and there was literally hundreds of mixtapes out every month. Big Mike, DJ Whoo Kid, Kay Slay, they were dropping mixtapes like every two weeks. You'd always be logging on and downloading them, so of course

Shoot 5 Ent. presents
Dirty South G's Vol.34

Shadyville and Paperview Media present DJ E Stacks
Welcome to Trilla Delphia 9

DJ Sam.G presents
Street Furious Pt.3

DJ Soulless & Vendetta Mixtapes
Traps R Us Vol.8

Shoot 5 Ent. presents
Dirty South G's Vol.31

Shoot 5 Ent. presents
Dirty South G's Vol.33

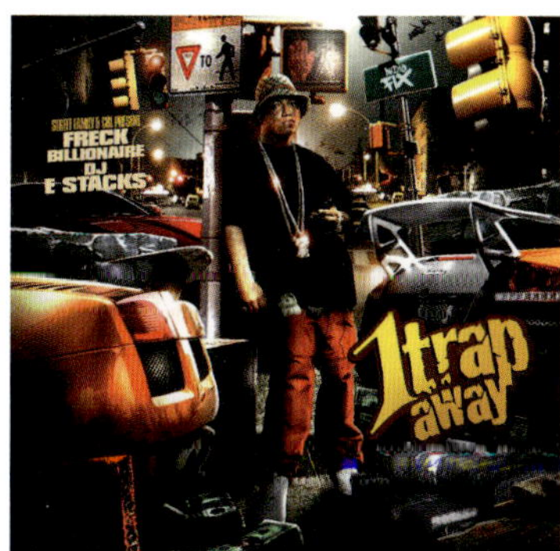

DJ E Stacks & Freck Billionaire
1 Trap Away

Shoot 5 Ent. presents
Heavy In The East Vol.24

Aphilliates present Willie Da Kid, LA The Dark Man &
DJ E Stacks – *Repo Men*

Shoot 5 Ent. present Young Jeezy
The Trap Leader

DJ E Stacks
Audio Fix Part 12.5

DJ Gutta Mixtapes presents
Who Wants To Be An MC 7

Young Lex
Cold Night In The Summer

Shoot 5 Ent. & The Empire presents
ATL 13

T.I.
Trap Back Jumpin

T.I., Yo Gotti & Young Jeezy
Hustle 101

Gunplay
The Best of Gunplay

T.I., Yo Gotti, & Young Jeezy
Hustle 102

Shoot 5 Ent. presents
Dirty South G's Vol.32

DJ Big Headline & Waka Flocka
Gangsta Nerd

DJ Starks
Frontline Gunnas Vol.1

DJ Blazita & Freck Billionaire
Terrorizing the Streets

T.P.
Champaign's Most Wanted

Shoot 5 Ent.
Heavy In The East Vol.13

Traps R Us
2 Gunz Up

DJ Scream & Shoot 5 Ent. presents
Heavy In The East Vol.6

Shoot 5 Ent. presents
Heavy In The East Vol.17

Love Dinero
Brick Squad Music – Supa Turnt Up

French Montana
Shot Caller

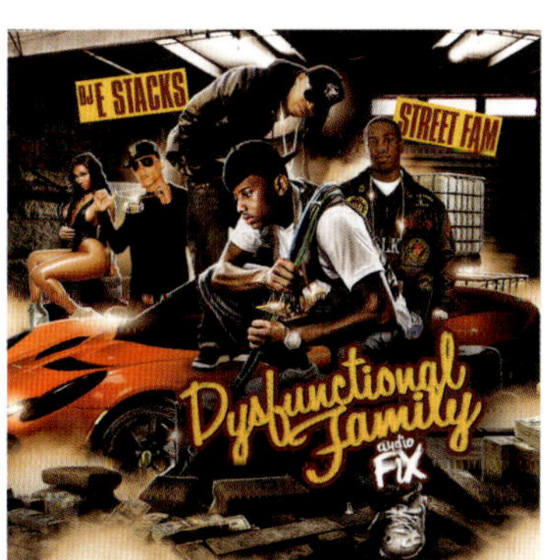

DJ E Stacks & Street Fam
Dysfuncational Family

Digital Product, DJ Gutta & DJ Lazy K
Brick Squad Unloaded – We Run These Streets

DJ Playboy
iRegulate Vol.3

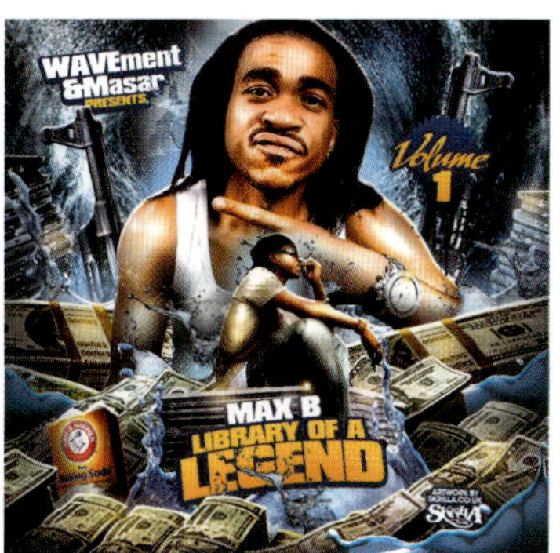

Wavement & Masar presents Max B
Library Of A Legend Volume 1

C-Brown
Thugacation – Born Dead

G.I. The General & French Montana
Henny & Sour

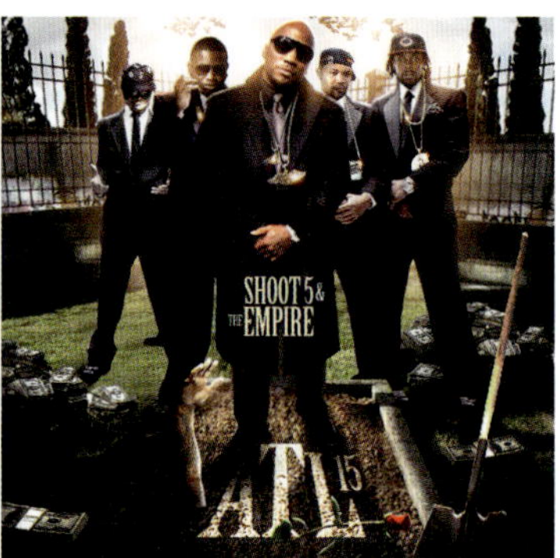

Shoot 5 Ent. & The Empire
ATL 15

you'd have these new covers and stuff. It was the same time that 50 Cent and G-Unit came out. Obviously, they were the pioneers in bringing the mixtape thing into the forefront.

You mentioned how it used to be easier to get in touch with DJs or artists through the internet in the past. How do you get work nowadays?

Most of my work comes via word of mouth, really. I've been doing this for six or seven years now, so I think my name is somewhat established. Most of my work comes from recommendations or people just seeing my work in various places. I don't tend to advertise too much. Obviously I've had my website up so people can look at my portfolio. But I don't make too much of a point to advertise or actively seek for jobs. Most of my jobs tend to come to me, which is good. I'm quite lucky to be in that situation.

Over these six or seven years, how would you say your visual style has changed?

A lot of the early stuff I did was trying to fit in with what other designers were doing. The main mixtape designer who inspired me was Nojo. His designs were amazing. I think he's very underrated among other designers. I don't know if it's a case of people not wanting to admit how good he is or that they were influenced by him. But I think every mixtape designer has been influenced by the covers that he used to do because his covers looked like movie posters. They were amazing. I remember when I first started out, I would try to emulate Nojo's covers. He's one designer that I have spoken to a few times and from reading about him and I know that he doesn't just do mixtape cover design. He also does advertising, he's a professional designer. Back then, I saw that he did mixtapes and that he also was a professional designer, so it was a huge influence on me to see that you can do both. It made me realise that mixtapes aren't an amateur thing. That you can bring professionalism into designing mixtape covers.

When did you start defining who you are as a designer?

I have established my own individual style in how I approach certain projects. I started to get a kind of momentum going in how I put together covers and I've reached a point where you can look at a cover and say *that's a Skrilla cover* or *that's a KidEight cover.* It can be things like certain sets of fonts and effects that we use. I think that's how my style has developed. I've developed my own style to where I use a certain set of elements. That gives me my own identity as a designer, that when people look at my covers they know who made it.

2 Chainz & Gucci Mane
Trap Gods

DJ Drop, DJ Fletch & Young Jeezy
Mr. 17.5

Serious Attributes Entertainment presents
Kontraband Material 2008-2012

Team Legends & Up North Records, DJ Krazee Rae, DJ King Ecko & Maxx B – *Lyfe After Brydgang*

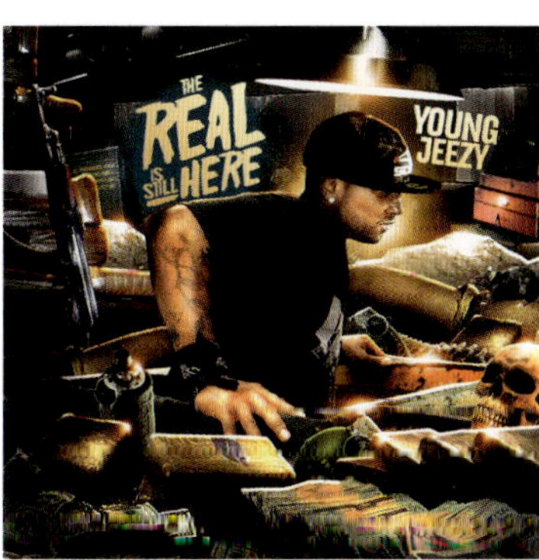

Young Jeezy
The Real Is Still Here

Urban Jones
The Rush and the High

How would you define that identity in a few words?

It's flashy. It's in your face, larger than life and it grabs your attention I guess. I also would like to say that it's clean, through the way I work with highlights and shadows. It's impactful and attention-grabbing but it doesn't overwhelm you. You can identify all the individual elements when you look at it. It's not overpowering to you but it's still a powerful image. That's a good aspect of clean design.

When did you feel like you'd developed your skill set in Photoshop?

I don't think you could ever master Photoshop. You could be really, really good at it but there is always something new you can learn. Every time a new version comes out they bring new elements, new filters and stuff. It does come in handy but I think if you rely on it too much, it takes something away. It doesn't add much to your designs, it only save you time. To begin with, you need to be a good designer.

Is your process fully digital or do you also sketch by hand?

When I was at university, they taught us to sketch by hand and I used to do that when I first started out. But now I don't. I start on the screen. In a way, initially when I create a design and I'm playing around, it's like I'm sketching in my head. I'm creating the image myself using elements that I already have, creating a collage. So no, I never really put pen to paper, not nowadays.

Is that because you're most comfortable working digitally or because it's just time-saving?

It's both. With a project like a mixtape cover, you're not really going to sit down and sketch out an idea or put a lot of that process into it. Unless it's a huge project. That kind of outlines the difference between the mixtape design industry and other graphic design industries. If you work for a company and get a brief from a client, they would expect to see images sketched out, moodboards, creative processes, and things like that. But the mixtape industry's turnaround time is a lot quicker and the money is different, so obviously the creative process is gonna be somewhat different.

On average, how much time do you spend on a cover?

It can vary. It doesn't take as long as it used to. When I first started out, I could sit for five or six hours on one cover, trying to get it right, and it probably didn't look very good

Gucci Mane & DJ Below Zero
I Go Hamburglar

Rastamat aka Jeune Ras
Ras Krispies

Wala
Magic Trix

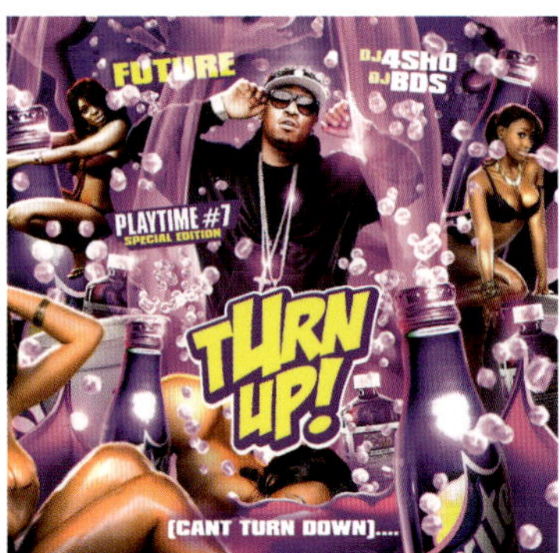

Future, D 4Sho & DJ BDS
Turn Up! (Can't Turn Down)...

DJ Woogie, Shiest Millini & Gotham Gang
God Forgives Doeboys Don't Vol.1

Love Dinero
Gucci 2 Time

Three Six Mafia
Traps R Us Vol 7

DJ Fletch & Lil Debbie
Keep It Lit

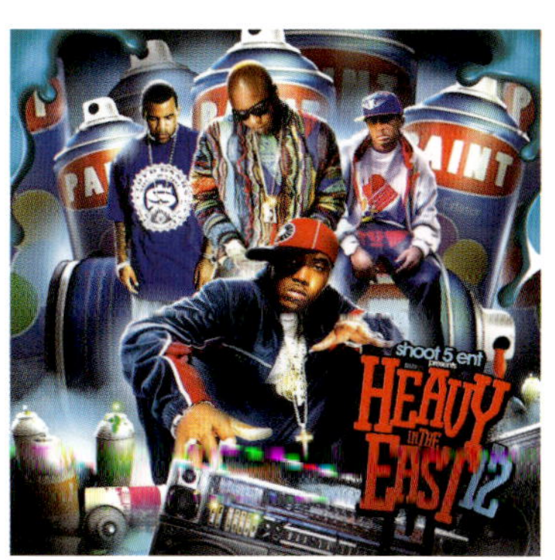

Shoot 5 Ent. presents
Heavy In The East Vol.12

The Yo Gettaz Hustle Team presents DJ Scratchez
Out Of This World Hitz – Welcome To My Hood Edition

Shoot 5 Ent.
This Is The Remix

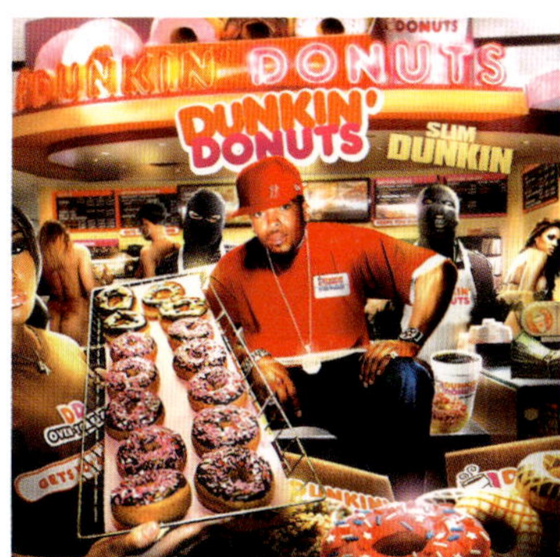

Slim Dunkin
Dunkin' Donuts

DJ Playboy
iRegulate 4

in the end but that's because I was learning how to do it. But I don't think it should take longer than a couple of hours at the most. Some of the best covers I've done were literally knocked out in an hour or something. I think that when you have the idea or concept hitting you straight away, you can sit down with Photoshop and pull it all together very quickly.

During your most creatively intense periods, how many covers have you produced?

It's hard to say. I've knocked out several in a day, maybe three or four in a day. Once, I must have done about 20 or 30 covers in about a week. It really does vary and depends on how much work I've got coming in. Sometimes I might just have one cover to do for a day. That's quite nice because I can sit back and I can really think about what I want to do, then put some proper time into it and it comes out really nice.

Regarding the relationship between the music and the cover art, do you find it important that they fit together?

It's quite interesting actually. A lot of the time, we designers don't get to hear the music before we start on the project. For various reasons, obviously. Sometimes the music is not finished. Other times, an artist isn't going to send his designer some music he hasn't released yet, for copyright reasons, I guess. But I think it works in both ways. Sometimes when you need a concept to work on, listening to a song really does help because it gives you a direction to go in. But other times, you don't really need to hear the music. If you got the title of the mixtape or a song, you can let your imagination go with it or you can develop a brand new image yourself. A lot of times, you want the cover to grab someone's attention, so the most important thing is that it looks good. If you look at mixtapes out there, there are some great cover designs where the music behind it is terrible. Sometimes it's even good that you don't hear the music so you just use your own creativity and do what you want.

Do you prefer creative freedom or do you like limitations?

Both can be nice but I think it's most creatively challenging when you have a title and a picture and you can let your imagination fill in the white canvas, which is a five by five inch square. And that's what your imagination is limited to, you got to fill this little square. It's great to be able to think that this title fills my head with all these ideas and you begin putting it all together. In the end when you see the finished cover on the screen, and it's what you imagined in your head, it's a great feeling. To have a creative concept and achieve it.

Can you tell us a bit about your creative process? Where do you start when you receive a job?

The client will email me the title and the picture or whatever. I think most of my original ideas are based on the picture I'm sent because it's great to work with a good photography. Depending on the style of the photograph, different poses, it completely changes the way I see the cover. If you get sent a picture of an artist's face, you are kind of limited. The way the cover is going to turn out is a lot different if you're sent an image of an artist sitting in a chair, or a full body shot. From the outset, you'll know what kind of cover you're dealing with and how much space you've got. So when I'm sent images like that, right away my brain begins to ask *how am I going to formulate this? How can I work this specific image into the cover?* So the pictures that I'm sent and the title is a huge thing for me.

Once that's established, I just start to play around and think about different colours and what elements I want to bring in. A lot of mixtape covers are very street so you need to think about what kind of other images you want to use. You can for example use money, women, guns and drugs, those kinds of things. Is it going to be a flashy mixtape? Or is it going to be a bit more laid back? Those things that get my creative thinking going.

What does your eye look for when blending elements together into one image? How do you make them all fit?

Initially, designers definitely struggle with making it fit. I know I struggled with it at first. Really, it's getting the blending, lighting, and colouring right, which is something that you can only do with Photoshop. The blending, the shadows and things like that are definitely the hardest parts. If you look at some amateur covers, that's what they're missing and the perspective is off, nothing is blended well, nothing looks like it actually belongs together. That's the key aspect to a mixtape cover, making everything look like it should be there.

You use a very consistent color palette. Please explain how you work with color.

That's something you get with experience. You realize that certain colours go together and certain ones don't. If you look at the color wheel, you can get a feel for which colours go with which. Obviously, in the *Doeboys* cover (see previous page, editors note), there are purples and blues and blacks that go together. But if you threw a random color like red in there, it might make it feel a little bit off. It's just about having an eye for design, really.

Growing up with comic books. Do you see any connection between comic book art and mixtape covers?

If you walk into a comic book store, there are so many things that grab your attention. The comic book covers are really great at doing that. That is definitely something that has influenced me. That impact of seeing a comic that make you think *I need to pick that up and look at that.*

Gotham Gang presents Shiest Millini, Wale & Chief Keef
Doe Or Die Vol 5

DJ Easy presents
Puerto Rico – A Tribute To Big Pun

DJ Gutta, DJ Capcom & DJ Decko
Mixtape Mercenaries

Life Music Entertainment & DJ Young Mase presents
War Games – Operation Shady

Burnt MD
The Green Invasion

Genius Moneky Group presents D. Money Chaser
Hottest In The City Vol 1

The World Wide Fleet DJs, Roxx Ruger & DJ Lexus
Cruel Intentions

Shoot 5 Ent. & The Empire
ATL 14

Thatshiphop.com presents DJ Green Lantern
Unsigned Invasion

Shoot 5 Ent.
Dirty South G's Vol.19

Shoot 5 Ent. presents Y.C, Future & Rocko
Watch This

Streetsweepers presents Papoose
Papoose Season

Darkage Ent. presents Tommy 2 Face
Time 2 Face The Music

Thatshiphop.com presents DJ Drama
3rd Infantry Division Part 2

Traps R Us, DJ Soulless & DJ Ransomdollars
Above The Law

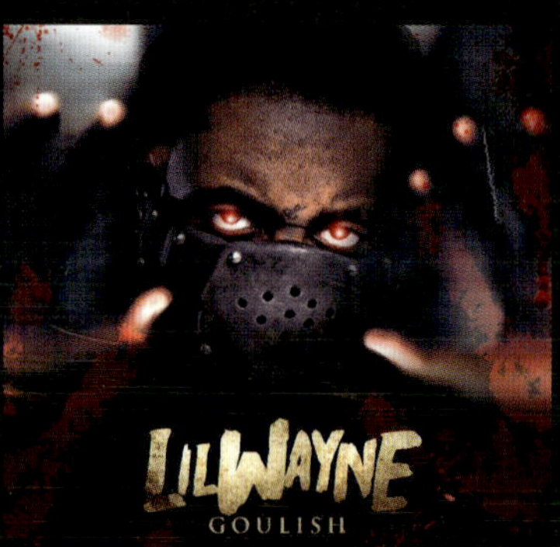

Lil Wayne
Goulish

Left
New Humans

Gotham Gang presents Shiest Millini, Ace Hood & Young Scooter
Doe Or Die Vol 6

DJ Wats & Gotham Gang presents Young Jeezy, 2 Chainz & Shiest Millini
Doe Or Die Vol 2 – The Order

Gotham Gang presents Wiz Khalifa, 2 Chainz & Shiest Millini
Doe Or Die Vol 3 – Game Of Thrones

DJ Fletch
Dubstep Attack 4

DJ Fletch
Dubstep Attack

DJ Fletch
Dubstep Attack 2

Would you say that comics influenced your mixtape work?

Yes, comics, to a certain extent, and movie posters. When it comes to composition, I think those are huge influences to most designers. The original mixtapes that came out, they were all based on movie posters. That was the trend of the time. People would take them and manipulate them and put rappers in them. I think it was because the majority of movie posters are properly composed images. The scale of the different elements, it just works. So when you're a designer, you take tips from what you see and you imitate that kind of layout. You can learn a lot by browsing movie posters. That's one of the best things a designer could do. Just look at how they put things together, where the texts goes, how the text is formulated together with the images. If absorb what you see in movie poster, you can bring that into the mixtape or CD cover game.

Do you have any favourite movie posters?

The *Dark Knight* posters are really good, with the composition and things. I think the *Tron: Legacy* poster is really cool. If you look at the way they use the light. They took the blue image, the blue glow and used it all over their campaign. It's very distinctive and it's a great thing to do because it all look very cohesive.

Are there any visual trends in mixtape cover artwork that you've seen and wanted to try?

I've seen them all, from being around since the very start of mixtapes. Artists are always going to be influenced by what's going on in the world. There are always going to be things that are trending or popular topics that people want to capitalize on. As I said the original trend was all about movie posters. Then everyone started using smoke. There were covers with so much smoke in them that it became ridiculous. Then there was a trend to have a moon and some birds in there. And then there was a trend to make everything look like a cartoon. There was also a period when everyone were using a Photoshop filter called *Lucy*. One designer used it and literally everyone went crazy for the next six months or a year over this little filter. It made the image look really grainy, really weathered and detailed. It was really strange. It worked great on some covers but others just looked awful because they'd overuse it, that always happens with trends.

Whenever an interesting trend comes along, you pick up on it and you're like *Oh, that's cool,* and you use it in some way. I think every designer is the same. We all follow certain trends. Sometimes it's not even our fault because if something's popular, the DJ or artist will say to us *I want it to look like this.* Clients often want something that is current and similar to what's out there at the moment.

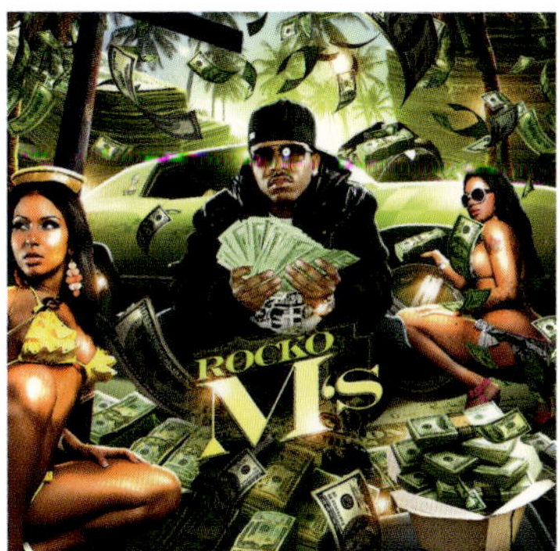

Rocko
M's

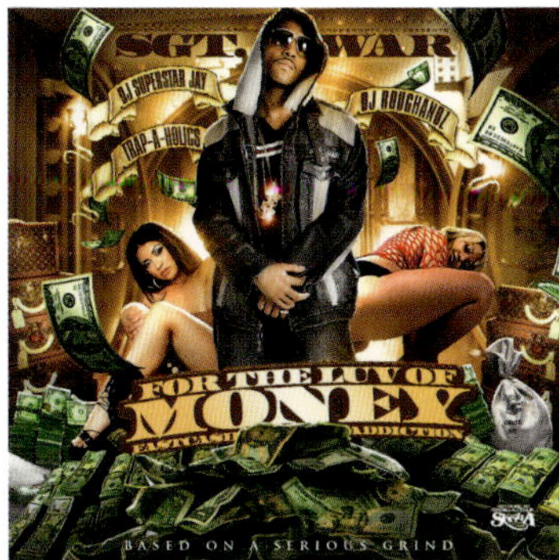

DJ Superstar Jay, Trap-A-Holics & DJ Roughandz
For The Luv Of Money

DJ E Stacks
Welcome to Trilla Delphia 7.5

Shoot 5 Ent. presents
Heavy In The East Vol.15

ABS Entertaintment & Prestijus presents Jus Superlor
Scared Money Don't Make Money – In HD

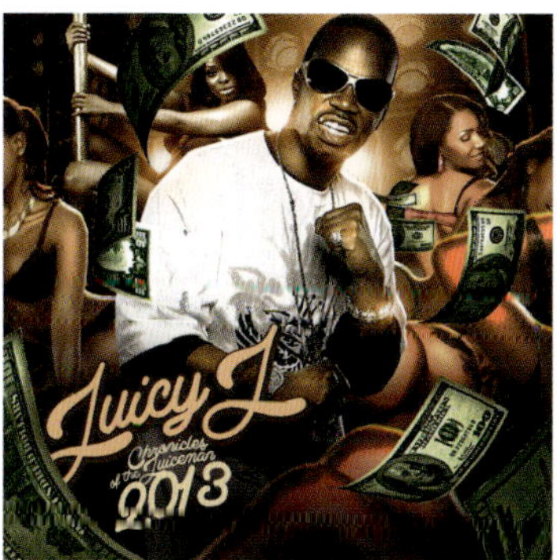

Juicy J
Chronicles of the Juiceman 2013

Do you have any examples of things you've done and seen other people pick up on?

That's interesting because I went on a website yesterday and saw someone who took my CD cover and badly Photoshopped some new text onto it, changed a few colours and were selling it as a new design. So basically they just bootlegged my cover, which is rather bad. I know that has happened to quite a lot designers. That's probably the worst case of when something like that has happened. I don't know who's done it. I'll probably never find out who did it, it's impossible. But there's nothing I can do about it because none of those images are mine to copyright anyway, which is an interesting aspect of what we do. We don't really have any copyright over our work. And with the internet, if people can't stop people bootlegging music, I'm never going to be able to stop someone taking my cover. So you can't get too mad at it.

How is your relationship to your fellow designers?

I speak a fair amount with KidEight. He's also an English designer, so we have that in common. When he first started designing, we used to speak all the time. I used to help him out with things, like how the taxes work. So he's one of my closest designer friends. On one hand, it's a competitive industry because it's so closed and there is not that many jobs. I don't think any designer is going to be great friends with another designer. But on the other hand, I guess we should be more of a close community. It does work both ways. There should be communication and we should be helping each other out because there is not many of us. But then it's quite competitive and there is only a certain amount of projects. I guess it would be hard to do. And especially since it's such a niche industry. It's not really looked upon as a great art form unless you're interested in it, so a lot of the designers are not given the respect they deserve. Therefore it's quite hard to tell clients that *these are the top designers, they are the people you should work with.* Similar to forming some kind of union. It would be great if that happens because if all designers were to join together and establish some kind of basis for what we do. Then things like minimum prices could be established and we would probably all gain from it.

I remember several years ago, my friend, who is a music producer, was talking to me about how there was no union or anything established for producers, so a bunch of them got together and made something where they would get credit and a certain amount of money for their production. It would be great if we, the designers did that too. The average price for a cover should be 200 dollars, but that's not always the case. It can really vary. But if something was worked out where we all got together and said *right, we're the best designers and we're charging a minimum amount of money.*

Yo Gotti
White Winter

DJ Soulless
Black Ink On Dead Presidents

DJ Dollar Bill, DJ Big Headline & Shawty Lo
Big Money Talk

Shoot 5 Ent.
Heavy In The East Vol.19

DJ Soulless
Cut The Check

Jim Jones
Rich Porter Back

Love Dinero & Waka Flocka Flame
Benjamin Flocka

DJ Fletch & Emondsta
Girls, Guns & Gold

DJ Fletch & King Cru Inc
The Afterparty

Shoot 5 Ent. presents
Dirty South G's Vol.37

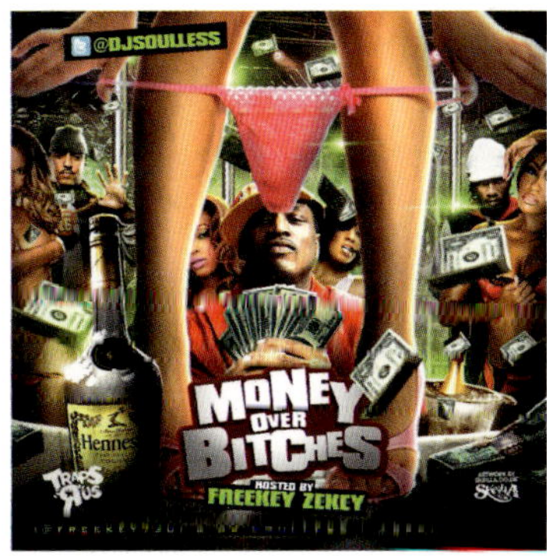

DJ Soulless
Money Over Bitches

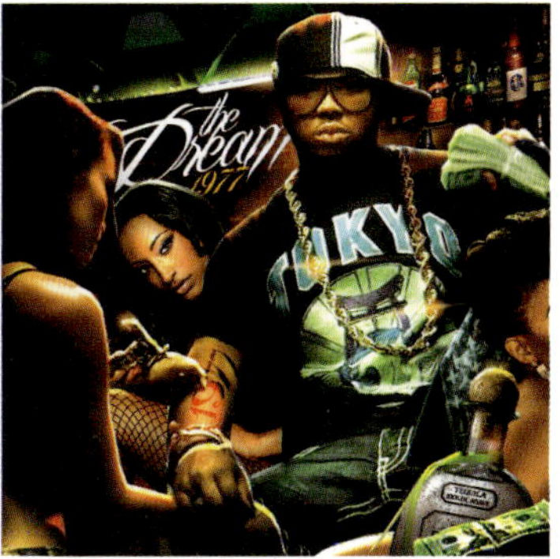

The Dream
1977

DJ Clark Blaze presents
High Notes – The Vito Genovese EP

Shoot 5 Ent.
Heavy In The East Vol.26

Future
Go Harder 3

Quest MCODY
King Cody

Shoot 5 Ent.
Heavy In The East Vol.10

Shoot 5 Ent.
Heavy In The East Vol.20

DJ Reese, Big Tobacco & Bun B
Too Trill for TV

Shoot 5 Ent. & The Empire
ATL 17

King Marvey X
F.O.E – Fresh Outta Exile Vol 1

Wale
Panamera Lifestyle

If you want our kind of quality, this is what you're going to pay. I think that would definitely take the mixtape design game a lot further.

Have you had any bad legal experiences?

Thankfully not. I think since what we do isn't very mainstream, it has worked in our favour. If our designs were everywhere and sold in regular shops, a lot of us would get in trouble. But that's one of those things designers don't really talk about because of the legal consequences.

Do you have any thoughts about the mixtape industry's transition to digital form?

It's great to hold a physical copy of what you've done in your hands. But now that the majority of mixtapes never will be printed that is happening less. You really appreciate it on a different level when you get to hold the object in your hands. It's a great feeling. Aside from that, it hasn't really changed the mixtape game too much.

Where do you think your work is heading?

I wouldn't really like to guess. Hopefully it improves and I can keep bringing in new ideas but I'm not really sure. I just want to keep doing what I'm doing and keep getting better at what I do. I think it might be heading in a direction where certain things are stripped down using a more clean and professional look. That's definitely something I will be looking at in the future. As I feel my work is going in that direction right now, I would like to take it further because I think that it's good if you can convey something really simply but effective. Some images from my work are very detailed but it doesn't always have to be that way.

If you would live one day inside the world of one of your mixtape covers, what would that day look like?

I think that would be a bit of a crazy day to be honest. A lot of women, a lot of money and a lot of drugs. Depending on what mixtape, it could take me from the most hostile environments or life threatening situations, to some high-class showbiz party. I don't think I'd want to be in some of these hoody environments. But I wouldn't mind being in some of the covers that have a lot of money in them. It would certainly be a rather crazy day. I guess that's part of the artform we do. It's not reality. We're taking elements of the music and reality and then bringing them into a larger than life image.

Could you pick a memorable cover and explain it? How it came about and how you came up with the concept?

I like *Columbia* by Young Scooter. That's quite an interesting cover for a mixtape done for a DJ that had put together a lot of music from the artist Young Scooter. His main song was called *Colombia*. I received an email that simply said *Young Scooter, 'Colombia', Young Scooter on the cover*. And that was it. I wasn't too familiar with Young Scooter's music, I Googled it and found the song *Colombia*, it was helpful.

This is one of those covers where the music definitely influenced the design. Because after listening to the song, and reading the lyrics, I got an idea for where the mixtape came from. The cover is very much influenced by the lyrics in the song as It's all about drugs and drug trafficking in Colombia. I wanted to bring out images in a scene and convey those themes of drug money and drug trafficking. That's why I used the boat image in the background, the helicopters and the soldiers. I really wanted to bring out the atmosphere of the song. The idea behind it and tie it all together in the cover, which I think I did quite well. So I decided that I'd go in the direction of lots of drugs and money and guns, which isn't really unique in the mixtape game. But it's all about trying to take the same elements that a lot of people use but creating something unique. I've read about Colombia and the drug trade in the past, so I'm quite familiar with it and that definitely helped bringing the ideas about. I Googled images of cocaine and Colombia and I got a lot of images of cocaine bricks, money, things like that. I also had to get a good image of Young Scooter. I gathered those elements and slowly built up the basis of it, beginning with the foreground and then working things into the background. And since it involved trafficking, I brought in the image of a boat on a loading dock.

I also felt like bringing in these images of soldiers and people who'd probably be involved in drug trafficking. I guess this image makes a statement by pushing you to think about how all these drugs come into America. They're not coming in by themselves, are they? It's not easy to bring drugs into the country. It poses the question of how many of these shipments are occurring and how many they let happen. So the military presence in the cover is a bit of a political statement. That's what hiphop music talks about. It's not blatantly political but it deals with harsh realities that are overlooked, and that definitely influenced the design.

TThen, there's the girl. It looks like she's randomly put in there, but Young Scooter talks about how he fell in love with a girl from Cuba in his song. The lyrics goes *I can make cocaine. I just fell in love with a Cuban. I just left Colombia. Always making bricks, me and Hector.* So I felt like putting the girl in there. It's worth looking at the lyrics because there's nothing hidden in them. They're so blatant. It's easy to pick up the influence or the concept from the lyrics themselves. So the cover became sort of like a scene from a movie.
When everything was established, I worked on blending it in and adding certain lighting to the image. Then I worked on the colours that I wanted the scene. I used this bluish tint to reflect a night scene, which I thought worked well with the drug trafficking theme. Finally, I just had to add text to the image, which is something that I never want to overpower the image, it has to mix well and stand out at the same time.

Young Scooter
Columbia

Future
Go Harder 2

DJ Jmas presents
Area 51

A book by Tobias Hansson & Michael Thorsby

Project Manager	Sara Eriksson
Graphic Designer	Michael Thorsby www.michaelthorsby.com
Editor	David Matthew Olson
Proof readers	Jonas Grönlund & Anders Häger Jönson
Printer	Lösch MedienManufaktur, Wailblingen

A very special thanks to the designers featured in this book
KidEight, Miami Kaos, Mike Rev, Tansta & Skrilla

Further thanks to
Trap-A-Holics, Evil Empire, Mixtape Wall, Rob Markman & Tapemasta

Thanks to
Andreas Wendén, Stefan Grahl, Alex Marquetti & Erik Löfquist

A proposal to Koenig Books by Anne Davidian (Praxis Matters)

First published by Koenig Books, London

Koenig Books Ltd. At the Serpentine Gallery
Kensington Gardens, London W2 3XA
www.koenigbooks.co.uk

Printed in Germany

Distribution

Germany & Europe
Buchhandlung Walther König, Köln
Ehrenstr. 4, 50672 Köln
Tel +49 (0) 221 2059653
Fax +49 (0) 221 2059660
verlag@buchhandlung-walther-koenig.de

UK & Ireland
Cornerhouse Publications
HOME
2 Tony Wilson Place
UK – Manchester M15 4FN
Tel +44 (0) 1612 123 466
Fax +44 (0) 1752 202 330
publications@cornerhouse.org

Outside Europe
D.A.P. / Distributed Art Publishers, Inc.
155 6th Avenue, 2nd Floor
USA-New York, NY 10013
Tel +1 (0) 212 627 1999
Fax +1 (0) 212 627 9484
eleshowitz@dapinc.com

ISBN 978-3-86335-977-5